PIVOTS
FOR
CAREER
SUCCESS

PIVOTS FOR CAREER SUCCESS

UNLEASHING PEOPLE POWER

R. GOPALAKRISHNAN
R. SRINIVASAN

RUPA

Published by
Rupa Publications India Pvt. Ltd 2021
7/16, Ansari Road, Daryaganj
New Delhi 110002

Sales Centres:
Allahabad Bengaluru Chennai
Hyderabad Jaipur Kathmandu
Kolkata Mumbai

ISBN: 978-93-5520-115-7

Third impression 2022

10 9 8 7 6 5 4 3

Printed in India

Contents

UNDERSTANDING
THE CONTEXT

Preface

On 14 February 1990, the world saw a picture of the earth as photographed from the Voyager-1 spacecraft. The earth was receding from the camera mounted on the spacecraft and changed from a large object to a barely discernible speck. It was impactful because the speck was observed from a distance of six billion kilometres from earth. Since the earth was a mere dot, the picture was dubbed 'Pale Blue Dot'.

How is that for perspective? The impact was enhanced by Carl Sagan's rich and erudite voice. He reminded us that humans are a mere micro-speck on earth which in itself a speck suspended within an enormous planetary system. Sagan reminded us that our residential speck, the earth, has seen human ego in spades, resulting in dynasties, wars and pestilence. The earth speck has also seen waves of innovation delivering technological advances like no other planet has, at least to the best of our knowledge.

The coronavirus outbreak in 2020 has, of course, taught us several lessons. The cognoscenti have commented upon these lessons. A key feature of the commentary has been that a speck of a virus, too tiny for our minds to comprehend, let alone our eyes to see, held all of humanity to ransom. It was like a punishment meted out from heaven for mankind's excesses.

Inspired by this narrative, we open our book by offering a separate and distinctive perspective, one that is relevant to the theme of this work. The perspective is that after unravelling the visible mysteries, humankind's future will more and more depend on the invisible mysteries.

Man (we use the term 'man' and 'he' to mean man or woman, he or she) has learned well how to understand and gain control over visible and palpable things like water, air, soil, wood, hydrocarbons, metal and chemicals. During the last century, man has learned to harness invisible things like atoms, electrons, bacteria and nanoparticles. Such mastery over the visible and the invisible has delivered the benefits of industrial and electronic revolutions. This accounts for the sharp increase in human existence during the last 300 years.

Arguably, it could be stated that mastering the invisible has produced greater rewards compared to mastering the visible.

The more civilization advances, the greater becomes the role of human collaboration and societal understanding. This is perhaps the reason why management, as a profession, has advanced significantly during the last century. Management experienced its progress through the application of scientific and engineering techniques to improve efficiency and productivity of processes: from the genius of taking work to man rather than the age-old way of taking man to work, improvement of efficiency through industrial engineering to data processing, all the way.

The working of the human mind is among the last invisible continents waiting to be conquered. Sitting at the intersection of psychology and neuroscience, the scientific understanding of the human mind and its workings is currently at the early stages. The science is being experimented and uncovered. Despite all the apparent advances in brain science, experts acknowledge that neuroscience has barely gotten started.

The ways in which the brain works may be yet another invisible force with the potential to elevate or destroy human capabilities. That is indeed the central subject of this book.

As it has happened with much of science, the art of application long precedes the understanding of the science. Experienced managers are practitioners of understanding the human mind since they spend their career appreciating and learning what works and what does not, when it comes to human motivation and people. Industrial managers have practical experience of how we think and behave, irrespective of whether they are accountants or engineers. And this provides a backdrop to the authors getting together to write this book.

Throughout their professional careers, both authors have been corporate leaders in large, well-reputed organizations, leading and working with big teams of people. Together they have about 85 years of organizational experience—in Unilever, Tata, ITC and their allied companies.

Both have been fortunate to study at IIT (both from Kharagpur, by the way) and have been privileged to receive the finest and most intensive of external and in-house leadership programmes. Therefore, neither is innocent of the labyrinthine jargon used in business and management.

Both rose well in their companies to the CXO suite. They have real experience of what it takes to clamber up the slippery grease poles of corporate careers. In the process, they have developed a distinctive view about business careers and leadership. They bring together an elemental view of the subject as also an incisive view—from the hot, dusty environment of markets and factories to the terrace view from the dizzying heights of the well-carpeted board rooms.

This book is born out of so much about who the authors are, or more accurately, who they have been. Their diverse experiences provide the lens through which their world view is constructed. After all, there is no reality—perception alone is reality!

Many of the subjects in business management can be taught—like economics of business, finance, marketing, selling, productivity and efficiency and the regulatory environment of business. These are all subjects of instruction at business schools. Once such a body of explicit knowledge is learnt, application and experience act as the finishing school for the up-and-coming manager.

Management is all about people—about how we think and interact. People relations is one subject that must be learnt lifelong. It is a mysterious subject. It is not the preserve of the HR department—unlike Quality, Accounting and Marketing. People relations is the agate mortar on which the pestle of management excellence is grounded.

People relations must be honed on the anvil of experience on the job. Unlike any of the other subjects of relevance, a manager must learn the subject day-by-day, every day of the career. Young managers have real questions, for example:

- How outspoken should a young manager like you be?
- Should you plan your career or leave it to the company?
- Should you be perceived as a loyal subordinate or a questioning and engaged colleague?
- What should you do with office politics?
- What if you get a nasty boss?

This book is not about answering these questions seriatim. It is about the broader cloud in which those questions reside; it's what we have termed as 'people relations'.

There are no hard-and-fast rules about answering such questions. There are only rich, personal experiences of well-travelled managers, and they provide a compass to learn the lessons of experience.

The authors started out trying to capture the lessons of their experiences, to narrate the several lessons that they had learnt, bolstered by relevant stories and anecdotes. As they talked about the subject, they realized that they could end up spouting motherhood- and-apple-pie statements because the lessons could appear to be self-evident. Even if written in an engaging manner, would the reader relate to them? Upon reflection and delving into their respective careers, they realized that perhaps they must take a top-down as well as bottom-up approach.

When you are in your late 60s, every lesson of life appears to be obvious. But how often did you overlook these elementary lessons during your climb up the grease pole? Many, many times.

It just happens that the authors are blood brothers, some six years apart. They climbed different escalators in different organizations, but each had a ringside view of the other's journey, a privilege only a brother can have. Together, their years of experience add up to a lot—they represent a cauldron of some very valuable lessons.

The companies that they worked in are endowed with solid, well-established management development systems, and with as competent an HR function as you can encounter anywhere. At a macro level, there are many similarities in their world view about careers, but there are subtle differences as well. These differences emanate from assumptions that one acquires in organizations, which are endowed with cultural givens.

Indeed, on the occasions when they engage with young people about careers, they find that they are enamoured, but not obsessed, with vision, strategy, technology and transformation. They are hassled with questions, such as, how many jobs they should change, how they should deal with difficult bosses, how they should plan their career and how they should cope if a colleague gets promoted to be their boss.

In other words, they have direct and simple questions, devoid of the complexity that senior people are engrossed with. Although their questions about careers are indeed simple, the answers and approaches display a wide range of options. There is no one-size-fits-all solution. It is this aspect that the authors have decided to try and capture in their book—the cloud in which these questions reside, the cloud of how people think and act.

The book does *not* offer young students and career-makers a standardized, do-it-yourself set of solutions, but suggests ways to think about the problems related to relationships and careers. The authors have adopted an approach of talking intimately with the reader. They averred that their narrative could then be interesting. There are many pat problem-solution career lessons available, but fewer lessons on how to think about the way people think and act.

That is because all books are biased by their respective authors' experiences. Here are two authors with different experiences in different companies. They wrote them independently but devised a practice of arguing about the lessons. Their narrations read differently; indeed they are different. But they bear a unified lesson about human nature. No lesson that they write about will come through as so obvious that it would not even be worth noting! They might have included 100 lessons if they had not adopted this filter.

As authors, they are like new parents. They really love what they have created. But that may not be what the reader will feel. They think that this is not a book to be read in one go on a flight between cities. This book is more like a bottle of wine, to be savoured in small sips, tossed around in a swirl, and allowed to flow through, quietly and with warmth. When we have traversed the long journey of a career, we view our early steps quite differently as compared to when we were living them. They provide learning just in the same way as adults learn from childrens' stories!

As adults, we tend to discount the lessons from children's stories. This has been commented upon in a delightful magazine article.[1] Ignoring books like *The Little Prince*, *Alice in Wonderland* and *Panchatantra*, when one is an adult and capable of rereading them from a more mature standpoint, could turn out to be a serious mistake. For example, in *The Little Prince*, a boy prince falls to the earth from the sky and visits many funny people during his travels on earth. There is a red-faced gentleman, who has never smelled a flower because he had been busy letting people know that he is a serious man! There is a lamplighter, who does the same thing all the time, day after day, because those are his orders!

Through the stories of their climbing days, maybe they could create the archetypes of experiences that even more experienced managers could recognize from their own repertoire.

At the end of their long career journey, the authors have stumbled upon the most elementary truth: it is very difficult

---

[1]Maria Konnikova, 'What Grown-ups Can Learn from Kids' Books', *The Atlantic*, 6 August 2012, https://www.theatlantic.com/entertainment/archive/2012/08/what-grown-ups-can-learn-from-kids-books/260738/.

to judge oneself, to judge others and to judge the context in which we interact with others. And that is why we have written this book. The authors hope the reader enjoys it, shares the lessons and lives the anecdotes.

Enjoy the read and the journey.

∽

UNDERSTANDING
SELF

Listen to Your Body

 It is in the first 10 years after the beginning of a working career that the greatest neglect of youthful health begins. Sportsmen stop playing sports, teetotallers drink alcohol, non-smokers smoke, active youngsters sit on desk jobs and starving hostel inmates eat rich food. These early years are the ones to watch.

You can convince yourself of the reasons—lack of time to exercise, the importance of socializing, the difficulty of getting a club membership, timings, logistics of travel and work and a whole host of other explanations. However, even if all these are correct, you can always go for a walk or do yoga! There are no reasons good enough for lack of fitness and exercise other than indulgence and laziness.

While growing up in Calcutta (now Kolkata), I joined tennis coaching at the Bengal Lawn Tennis Association. It was run and supervised by Dilip Bose, the Indian Davis Cup tennis star of the 1940s. He was a fiend for fitness. Before we could get our tiny hands around the racket, he would make us run around the South Club tennis court 10 times, do 100 jumps with a skipping rope, and do another 50 sit-ups. We were too tired to play any tennis by the time all this was done. His message was that we could not be tennis players if we were not fit. There is much truth in this for executives. The stereotype shown in advertisements of the high-living and high-spending executive is completely mythical.

One day, Dilip Bose asked us, 'How would you take care of your car if you were told that it would be the only car you would have for your entire life?' The answer was self-evident; all of us kids said the same thing in chorus.

'Well, your body is the only car you will have for all your life. You cannot change it, so look after it like your only car,' he bellowed.

To a kid, that was a simple message to understand and to remember. I owe it to the late Dilip Bose that I grew to love exercise and tennis, both of which have been an inexhaustible source of pleasure, relaxation, character-building and fitness, all rolled into one bundle.

Upon arrival in Mumbai for my first job, an early expenditure was on a membership of the Bombay Gymkhana. The club membership took precedence over the purchase of a motorcycle, music system or the occasional eating out.

It is terrific to see the number of gymnasiums with health-conscious executives exercising and keeping fit. A management career is extremely stressful, and every young executive should work at managing that stress. If you cannot manage your own health, weight and stress, how will you manage your factory or sales region?

Some people are unlucky because they develop natural health problems without bringing it upon themselves. But many others squander away their health on the grounds that office work is stressful. Healthy and young people need not develop stressful social habits by deluding themselves that they are relaxing. Such a hectic lifestyle catches up after 10 years.

My university tennis buddy was already a state-level champion. I used to wish I had his ground strokes and his swing. When I met him after 40 years, we naturally spoke about tennis. 'Oh, I gave up 20 years ago. I should have taken better care and played more regularly after college. I should have controlled some of my habits. I had to stop after a bypass surgery several years ago,' he said to my great regret, for he was such a lovely hitter of the ball.

I am not suggesting a Spartan lifestyle, far from it. Go out and enjoy life, youth comes only once. However, do listen to what your body is telling you and do not flog it to capacity.

Your good health is an asset on your balance sheet. Grow it, maintain it and do not destroy it. It is the only opening balance of asset you get at the beginning of your life.

∞

 Our parents and elders took care of us in our formative years, building habits of hygiene, sensible eating with balanced nourishment and regular exercise to keep fit. At school, a PT teacher often took on the mantle of taking us through free arm exercises, stretching and bending and running to sustain minimum levels of fitness. Those playing sports got specific exercises to tone up muscles and build up stamina.

Yet, what is easy and simple in teenage years drifts into jokes and negligence with the passage of time. Our confidence adds a 'devil-may-care' dimension in the hope that time can be made up later. Young working professionals feel aloof and mildly dismissive of those who complain of aches and pains.

At any number of seminars and lectures, people in the audience nod their heads wisely at the insights shared and then switch off as the next urgent phone call jerks them back to the normal habits of postponement of such irritating topics.

Yoga is mentioned nowadays as a holistic regimen that can be adapted for every individual, irrespective of age and constitution. A fitness band can monitor distance walked, blood pressure and frequency of exercise. Gyms offer a variety of modern equipment and personalized coaching for those interested. Some gurus offer an integration of breathing-physical-meditative exercises to keep body and mind in equilibrium. Ayurveda, naturopathy and homeopathy offer alternatives to allopathy, and some offer periodical body servicing to restore health. There is a continuous flow of advice on TV channels and the internet on what is good for you and what needs to be avoided and the advantages of moderation. A variety of equipment is on offer for slimming. New instruments are available for measurements of blood pressure and blood sugar. Home collection of blood, urine and stool is offered as a part of diagnostics with reports sent by email and updates available on a downloadable app.

Professional sportspersons, athletes and cinema stars are highly motivated to keep fit. Some have an interest in plastic surgery to continue to look young. There are many executives who follow a set routine and do quite well at cycling, half marathons, power yoga, workouts or regular walking.

Many people tend to take their bodies and minds for granted until breakdowns become serious enough. Then they rush to an expert for solutions. There are solutions. But the results are not always flattering or they are push-button solutions.

The finest resource is yourself—your body and mind! Why should you abandon these to external programming only?

Perhaps you have not developed the habit of taking

responsibility for yourself and to strive for continuous improvement throughout your life. Most people do not realize that they have been pre-programmed by somebody or the other, even if with good intentions. The moment this stimulus is withdrawn and full freedom is given to the individual there is a drastic fall in continuity and the individual tends to revert to a default setting of neglect, hoping for the best against breakdowns. The preventive aspect has not influenced the mind strongly enough.

Youngsters are often advised that when they start their professional career they will gain maybe a kilo a year for the next 30 years. You cannot defy the ageing process. Much can, however, be done to slow weight gain. Company appraisals rarely focus on health, and on the actions the individual takes to achieve 'fitness for purpose'. Company-sponsored fitness programmes and quick yoga, work for a short while, but fall by the wayside as other preoccupations crowd the agenda.

This approach inevitably affects the family, which juggles to balance work-life, eating out, entertainment and travelling. People fall into the same old trap and make subconscious assumptions that good health is not the immediate priority at such a young age, and can be made up later. This is not true, especially for family members who are away from company-sponsored programmes and feel these learnings do not apply to them!

Safety Mindset

At companies, safety and health measures are at least enforced. But not so in our personal lives. The coronavirus episode has taught us many lessons about safety and health. Think of what happens in good companies.

We know enough to integrate safety with health; we know how to use data analytics to drill down medical data to help fitness for purpose. The present data already shows back and neck vulnerabilities for those working on computers for long periods of time. We know slippages and falls can be arrested on the shop floor with better housekeeping and training drills for climbing up and down the heights. Fall arresters are essential for working at heights. Hard hats and safety helmets are *de rigueur* for those on two-wheelers and even away from work spots. Many who drive cars do not wear safety belts.

Drunken driving or use of a cellphone while driving is dangerous behavior that needs to be corrected, even outside the work area. Goggles are compulsory for welding. Radiation dosages need to be checked from time to time by monitoring personal badges. Safety shoes are essential on the shop floor and at construction sites. Ear plugs are essential in high noise or decibel areas. Truck drivers or helpers should not be allowed to snooze under their trucks at parking bays and inclines. Fire drills and evacuation drills should be made compulsory in every office and factory and restaurant. Fire exits should be periodically checked out without materials obstructing safe and speedy evacuation. Ramps, railings and toilets should be provided for those with special needs, over and above making designs more inclusive and safe.

All employees should be given refresher training in First Aid and the use of personal protective equipment (PPE) should be encouraged. Every meeting, *irrespective of the level*, should start with a brief safety pause, where people can relate a near miss at work or at home or outside or speak about a specific safety incident or near miss or accident that others should know about too.

If the above sounds like a laundry list, some of that is

inevitable, as a checklist is essential to cover several areas across a wide span of activities covering large numbers of people.

Haven't we all coached children on Diwali crackers, precautions while crossing the road, getting off a train/vehicle, safety belts, gas cylinders and slippages on escalators? We are concerned about the well-being of every person. The body is the only car that the person will have for the all their lives. We need to be free of avoidable accidents even as we strive to keep fit for a lifetime. Such aspects cannot be left to specialists alone.

ITC's Paperboards & Specialty Papers Division did not have a good safety track record in the mid-90s. DuPont shared some of their experiences at reducing accidents to near zero and preemptively building safety into all construction sites where contract labour was involved. Taking the senior management of the Paper & Paperboards business into confidence, a change programme was launched. This included giving Safety Officers at the four units in India wide responsibility and authority and investing the chief safety officer, Prakash Phatak, at Hyderabad, with responsibility for coordination, audits and sharing of findings across all sections and levels. CCTV cameras were installed in all areas for the first time in ITC (in non-security/non-gatehouse areas) with the objective of improving safety for all. These could be viewed from remote sites with Internet.

Work practices could be randomly supervised for accident hazards and snapshots taken of non-conformances, incidents/timing for follow up. The Union was taken into confidence that the purpose was not to spy on people but to ensure safe practices were followed and fatalities and bad accidents eliminated. Photographs taken were used again in training programmes to illustrate where non-conformance was endangering human lives. The idea was to move from lectures to specific safeguards that could prevent accidents and hazards.

As a result, accidents came down and the track record on safety and health steadily improved, despite heartbreaks in-between. It was decided to apply for the British Safety Council Sword of Honour, though amidst much diffidence and managerial scepticism. Finally, that milestone was crossed too in 2009–10. This award put the company's paperboards and specialty papers business on a much higher level of confidence and performance, which in turn boosted morale across all four units.

We need to safeguard our bodies and ensure safety for ourselves and our families and those whom we work with and meet. We need to build health and fitness into our lives. We need to focus sensibly on preventive maintenance and not rely only on breakdown maintenance!

∽

Find Fun in Work

A career means different things to different people. To some, it is an end point, a statement of ambition—for example, 'I must become the CEO of this company'. To others, it means the landmarks on the way—for instance, 'I must become regional manager in two years and general manager in three years thereafter'. To most, it is a combination. However, these are all destinations and not the journey.

To the wise, a career means the enjoyment and experiences of work. A career is not a destination; it is a journey.

What kind of a journey must you have? The answer is, 'A journey which you enjoy'. You can excel with consistency only at tasks that you enjoy doing. Roger Federer cannot imagine life without tennis, as much as Sachin Tendulkar cannot imagine life without cricket. Conversely, you cannot excel with consistency at tasks that you do not enjoy.

Enjoyment does not mean that the task is easy, or that you know how to do it. In fact it's quite the reverse. You enjoy doing things that challenge you sufficiently, yet are instructive to you. That engage you—for example, selling to a difficult customer, debugging a production issue, configuring a cost-effective solution to a problem and so on. It is engaging to you for your own reasons; some others may hate the same tasks.

Dev Lahiri joined Hindustan Unilever Limited (HLL) as a young manager in sales and marketing. He had studied in an excellent school, had a fine degree from a great college, was intelligent and articulate and had cleared a tough series of HLL interviews. He had all the characteristics to become a successful manager in the sales/marketing division. However, recruiting and developing managers merely through professional characteristics is fraught with risks.

One of the preparations before he could be assigned his first responsibility was field training. This meant that he had to work on a salesman's beat with an experienced salesman for 16 weeks. This involved visiting grocery shops and booking orders all day long, day after day. The idea was for him to learn the routine, pain and tribulations of a salesman.

Dev Lahiri was miserable. He found it boring, in fact, he considered it 'demeaning.' After spending some time with him, his boss wondered whether Dev would ever make a good sales manager. That did not *per se* make him a good or a bad manager; it just meant that Dev had to rethink what kind of work he should do to enjoy himself. The HLL job was quite a prized one: getting it was prestigious. Conversely, not being successful was considered by many to be a negative.

As Dev thought about it, something kept telling him that he had joined HLL just to prove to the world how smart he was and the salary had been a huge added attraction. It was not that he understood this career, and that he wanted to try it.

What he truly enjoyed was to spend time with school students—telling them about things they did not know, and some things that they might never know. He wanted to be a school teacher! Implementing his wish meant sacrifices of salary and image, among his family and peers. He was courageous and took the plunge.

I met Dev Lahiri 20 years later. By now he was the headmaster of the Lawrence School, Lovedale, a prestigious public school, probably earning a fraction of what he might have if he had stayed on at HLL. He was really enjoying himself, doing all sorts of new things at the school. And those gave him a sense of satisfaction. He told me that he had found his calling, his journey had been exciting, and he looked forward to each day as the sun rose.

Dev Lahiri had understood what a career meant—doing what you enjoy and enjoying what you do. Dev had realized that what was important was the journey, not the destination.

It is a pity that he died a few years ago—in my opinion, a great loss to the world of education.

∞

 Do you recall phases in school and college where you enjoyed some subjects and others not as much? Invariably, this influenced the attention we gave to the subjects over time. The reasons could have something to do with the teacher, our liking of the subject or a difficulty that one had not got over. The effect is the same—less interest and attention over a period to subjects that we do not enjoy, at least initially.

We are constantly learning over a lifetime, far beyond the formality of a classroom and the lecture or case study. Learning is not always linear or smooth but often takes place through adversities in non-ideal situations and sometimes through sharp discontinuities and unanticipated events.

I was chatting with some college friends at breakfast,

whom I had met after over four decades. There was nostalgia in the air and we obviously discussed professors we had known and had a laugh imitating some of them in good humour. Many of them had passed away and we felt a twinge of regret since they had left a mark on our lives and we had often lacked appreciation for them as human beings, managing in the circumstances of their days.

Dilip: If we were to assemble all of us in class again after all these years and ask what career you had envisaged 50 years ago, the disparity of answers will be amazing!

Rajaram: That's very true. There were chance factors at every stage that pulled us in unexpected directions.

Sankar: I never imagined I would work for a TV manufacturing company to start with. We had never seen a TV in our hostels!

Due to the conditioning in schools and colleges and the lecture system, we expect linear opportunities throughout life. This expectation tends to assert itself in subtle ways. We tend to have ideal expectations from our teachers that they must be competent, yet kind and affectionate under all circumstances.

This undergoes change in higher studies and professional college where we find wide diversity. Some are knowledgeable but not the best of teachers. Some are helpful and kind but not at the cutting edge of research. Some *were* excellent but have faded away with the passage of time. Some are incomprehensible, some irascible with mundane doubts being asked but unexpectedly good at cracking challenging problems. Some seem to have lost their way and you wonder how they got to where they are despite good credentials. What are some of the lessons we can draw from these diverse experiences?

The golden rule is: enjoy what you do and do what you enjoy!

The reader may sense a snag in such advice. Life is a bundle of subjects and activities, not all of which may be equally enjoyable. We revel in some, like a duck takes to water. Others are not so attractive. Some even seem distasteful. For example, I try football and injure myself while taking a slippery fall. This first experience colours my views and I keep off the game for a few years. Inducements to try football again do not impress me. I consider other sports as alternatives. Or choose other hobbies that interest me. Choices are narrowed down in some manner or the other of what I enjoy.

When it comes to school, we must appreciate that we are still expected to acquire a threshold of proficiency in subjects that we do not enjoy as much as others. The school system requires a broad familiarity with an array of subjects, with varied choices being given in the sciences, mathematics, humanities, languages and music, up to a certain class; specialization comes only later. The family subtly influences choices too.

The funnel narrows down further at college level and even further at the postgraduate level. There could be branching off at various points into other specializations and new opportunities. The professions that we join narrow our focus into more and more specific areas where our experiences shape our opinions. We, in turn, are influenced more strongly by the people we associate with more often. It is no surprise that an ENT specialist, a judge at High Court, a Vice Admiral, an entrepreneur in e-commerce and a music maestro may have all been classmates once upon a time in school.

Our choices are influenced by what we enjoy. We tend to do what we enjoy and correct our paths along our career trajectory when we prefer something else.

Try thinking of white sunlight broken up into a stream of colours by a prism and identifiable in the visible and invisible spectrum by wavelengths. The reverse seems more difficult. Can one stand at a specific wavelength and yet integrate all other wavelengths to get back sunlight without biases or filters?

Where does this leave us with respect to the lesson of this chapter?

There are multiple dimensions that we need to explore and gradually learn to enjoy as well.

There are opposite forces at work. We need to learn to enjoy more things that we do not usually enjoy or do that often, to push our boundaries further. The level of expertise may not be the same but even a modest improvement in skill and knowledge gives us a sense of intermediate mastery which is a source of satisfaction. It certainly increases the span of what we enjoy doing and encourages us to explore a little further to expand our envelope. This need not be a linear extension.

A nuclear scientist who enjoys music is not diminished at all. He can enjoy his research and his music too, as Albert Einstein and Homi J. Bhabha did. An artiste who dabbles in software programming may open new sources of satisfaction and enjoyment as Hindi film actor, Shammi Kapoor, did.

The fact that one chose a specific stream at a point of time need not deter them from exploring a new interest in a related or unrelated field at a later stage in life. In fact, such fusions can create new thoughts and streams of competence and unexpected new developments too.

Enjoy New Things

What we enjoy is not a static set of choices fixed in time.

We can deepen our understanding and competence in one area even as we broaden out to try other subjects and hobbies and pursuits that we enjoy to different degrees. These have a bearing on our attitudes and sense of well-being.

A Supreme Court judge shared that he enjoyed a course on mediation as it called for different skills than pronouncing judgements. He realized that adjudication had its limitations and did not deliver the best solutions to problems that two parties to a dispute could come to by themselves, with a little help and facilitation and unqualified listening. There was a great opportunity to resolve commercial and family disputes more quickly at lesser costs and with greater satisfaction for all concerned parties.

A friend told me that he experienced a sense of mastery and enjoyment from doing a set of courses offered online such as massive online open courses (MOOC). These can augment one's appreciation and enjoyment of even relatively rare subjects such as astronomy and black holes or spiritual philosophy. There are a host of YouTube lessons available for do-it-yourself improvements, including enhancing one's tennis or learning yoga or attending to car repairs or trying out new recipes or listening to TED talks. What seemed arcane and incomprehensible at a point of time, very often seems easier to read and understand in retrospect. The constraints on learning have been removed and one can learn from others by hearing, observing, practising, sharing, imitating and doing much more than what was possible before.

Our repertoire is constantly increasing and our sense of understanding and mastery continuously improving. We may surprise ourselves with our ability to learn on the go.

Recognize True Success

 Can a deeply involved person succeed without being passionate about his or her start-up or a new project or an innovative idea? The view is correct, but then crazy people also behave in a similar manner.

Passion is tested on the test bed of doing, making mistakes and learning all over again.

What is the difference between a passionate person and a crazy person? Adolf Hitler was passionate about creating a superior Aryan race for the progress of Germany, but for sure he was crazy. Blind passion is dangerous. It is touchy and sensitive about opinions, fallback and feedback. For success, sensitive passion must combine with good timing which, admittedly, has an element of chance or luck. Napoleon said he would always seek lucky generals, but for his brazen attack on Russia, at the Battle of Borodino, he did not have a lucky general. It is difficult to tell whether a person is obstinate or passionate because the behaviours can appear similar!

Passion is a surrogate for persistence and determination, the attribute of pressing ahead, suffering setbacks and hurdles, without cribbing.

Our family used to have a friend called Kumar. Kumar illustrates the dilemmas that arise from choosing an off-the-track path. Today, in his 50s, Kumar is a successful freelance film writer, director-producer of TV and feature films and has established a company to produce and direct feature films.

Kumar is a common bloke like any of us: the son of a retired judge, who has a sister and two brothers. Belonging to a middle-class, professional family, there was constant encouragement to study hard, qualify to join some profession and secure a job with a steady income. The elder sister and brother did just that. But young Kumar was different and restless.

He studied hard enough to pass. He graduated in commerce and even completed his articles for chartered accountancy with a top-notch accounting firm. He had done everything the way his parents wanted. Although he had studied diligently, he just could not see himself as a professional accountant. It was not his dream, and being an accountant was not even a door he wanted to knock on.

Deep within himself, Kumar felt a passion for something quite offbeat—especially so, for a middle-class family. He really loved watching Hindi films, and wanted to be a part of that world. When he saw Rajesh Khanna in *Anand*, he fantasized himself in that role. When he read Javed Akhtar, he imagined himself writing scripts. He indulged in his passions quietly and privately, all the while assuring himself that he had the talent.

For Kumar, films were fun. Success meant doing the best with what he had. So how could he not be successful? He could see only one way forward!

At 25, he announced to his family that he wanted to be in films. His father was aghast. But he was also sure that the young lad would dabble in it for a while and come running right back to join some firm as an accountant.

Kumar, B. Com, ACA, started a theatre group which allowed him to write scripts, act roles and direct plays. He virtually quit the world of commerce to follow his idea of great fun. It took seven years of struggle, but Kumar could not see any other way of leading his life. He was lost in this world he had created around himself; he enjoyed every moment. He chose which roles he would accept because his family supported him. If his family had chosen not to support him, he would have accepted lesser roles, but still in the field of film. The family support permitted his entry into films, and allowed him to follow one clear path forward with no alternatives! By his late 20s, his family saw clear evidence of Kumar's success. Kumar had acted in a TV serial called *Subah*, which turned out to be quite a commercial success. After that, there was no looking back. He is happy that he was single-minded about his passion—but he ensured that he developed the talent needed to be successful.

The great philosopher Thomas Carlyle once wrote 'Let each become all that he was created capable of being.' Kumar did exactly that, he followed his preferred path, suffered the vicissitudes, all the while demonstrating persistence and determination.

Here is a quotation from the offices of McDonald's that resonates with Kumar's case:

'Nothing in the world can take the place of persistence. Talents will not—nothing is more common than unsuccessful men with talent. Genius will not—unrewarded genius is almost a proverb. Persistence and determination alone are omnipotent.'

∽

 I remember feeling awed by my school's annual awards ceremony. Over the years, one has experienced many award functions, bigger than the school events. Trophies changed as they became bigger and better. The ceremonies became glitzier at corporate awards functions. I observed people receiving awards with due gravitas from the country's president on Republic Day. The gold medal of the Olympics or the august gathering at a Nobel Prize winning ceremony leaves one marvelling.

I asked myself: is getting an award a worthwhile goal, and should one get ready to shoot for an award? Then cringed, as I questioned myself: but how many people actually get it? Elders advised me that the striving was worthwhile, regardless of the prize. I heard stories of Mahatma Gandhi never getting the Nobel Peace Prize; also of Satyen Bose not getting a Nobel Prize for Physics, despite being immortalized in the Bose-Einstein statistics. Every time I won a match in sports, I was told not to get a swollen head but to aim higher for the next goal.

When I started working for a company after finishing my graduation, I was amazed at how the unionized employees pulled my leg. They told me in jest that management created incentive schemes and its primary goal was to raise the high jump barrier every few years. It made me introspect on the role of money and prizes as motivators. I struggled to find an answer that would apply universally.

As a senior manager and then as a CEO of a division and profit centre, I often wondered what would motivate younger managers who join the company. Every person is unique and different, yet we search for fail-safe policies that can ratchet up performance and fire up youngsters with motivation to pursue laudable goals.

If I were sitting in front of you, having a conversation on the subject, our exchanges may well resemble this:

You: Incentive schemes are okay, but don't always work.

Me: Of course, they need to be geared towards specific situations appropriately.

You: Doesn't the same apply to employee stock options?

Me: I think so, as they do not always work either with the passage of time or changing market conditions.

You: What happens in non-commercial enterprises?

Me: Power and recognition could be important factors here as well.

You: But that often involves long years of service, and there are no guarantees of success.

Me: Yet there are outstanding administrators, brilliant scientists, talented musicians, outstanding teachers and great contributors in all walks of life. They keep going!

You: What keeps them motivated to keep going and to succeed despite difficult odds?

Me: Abraham Maslow wrote about the hierarchy of needs, moving from physiological needs to love and esteem and then to ego and recognition and finally self-actualization

You: Does it really work in that order and sequence?

Me: Not perfectly, although it broadly holds true. There can be components of each need varying with time.

You: Some high-paying jobs involve incredible working hours, leaving little time for yourself or the family?

Me: Yes... And there is a burnout rate on health and family life.

You: Does it have to be this way or is there a balance that can be struck?

Me: I am sure there is a balance, although it may vary from person to person and situation to situation. One cannot be prescriptive.

At the end of these exchanges, we have touched upon several interrelated aspects of success but are, most likely, uncertain of what success factors contribute, when and for whom, and in what time frame.

Let us look at a small example of our experience with a new cell phone. The screen and features seem a little different but not so daunting as to discourage trial and experimentation. A few clicks or taps later, one feels better and postpones further exploration to a later date when there is less pressure of time.

When we find a quiet moment, one calmly tests out other features and can be absorbed in that challenge while travelling in a train or waiting at the airport. Half an hour goes by with little strain and one feels better already, ready to try out some outlier features that a friend had talked about enthusiastically. At each stage there is continuous learning and a growing sense of mastery and confidence: learning by doing.

Now, consider a musician or an aeromodeller or writer at specific instances of time, wrapped in concentration. The person looks forward to more such occasions as the feeling is irreplaceable and is its own reward. A child at play often displays similar absorption while playing with blocks or connecting a puzzle.

Magical Moments

- ◆ What is the magic that enables and creates such moments for individuals?
- ◆ Is it sustainable to the point that the experience lifts the entire population a little?
- ◆ Can there be more frequent experiences of this kind that make life enjoyable and productive despite irritations on other fronts?

External rewards or deterrents can work to a degree where traffic rules require compliance for the overall good. Where tasks are relatively routinized, there is a good chance of external incentives creating an atmosphere of predictability which may prove beneficial for all. This approach will not work where we need individual motivation to innovate and be creative or go the extra mile. Sometimes competition brings out the best in people, as sportspersons often exclaim after an intense match. The group in which one works can spark creative peer pressure to rise above the normal and deliver extraordinary performance.

Awards are often a culmination of such events and do have a part to play by way of recognition. They are not end goals and not ends in themselves, they are merely by-products.

We are all human and need some milestones along the way to keep running. We know instinctively that this is not an end goal but are human enough to enjoy the moment of recognition as a warm memory. The needs may vary widely from profession to profession or with respect to time. A film star may require more frequent affirmation in the early stages, a growing child may look forward to a moderate pat of encouragement to continue learning to walk (between losing balance every now and then), a scientist publishes a paper in a reputed journal which gets her recognition, a journalist draws a smile from an approving readership for putting across a difficult subject really well.

Is success in the 'doing' or in the 'getting'? The answer seems to be mixed. We know that affection is a critical factor in receiving approval and in promoting learning: what a child gets out of winning a sports medal or class proficiency prize; what a husband earns when a special increment at work draws a smile from the wife.

Psychologists Abraham Maslow and Frederick Herzberg, seem to speak to us. There is surely a hierarchy of needs, but there is a point where more of the same does not yield further results.

Money, for example, is an incentive, but pumping in more and more in the expectation of linear and proportionate improvement is unrealistic. The same holds good for awards. No human being likes being compelled to conform beyond a point, unless it is shown to be in the interest of the common good. No human being likes being manipulated or squeezed into a corner by a bully or a pernicious system.

Every human being feels he is capable of learning all the time and improving on-the-run and that he can contribute creatively and do something better than what prevails around him or what seems to be the standard that people have reconciled themselves to. The magic is working. Doing creates its own momentum in quiet and unobtrusive ways. Doing more sustains the enthusiasm to do even more, albeit, a step at a time.

There is far more success in the 'doing' than in the 'getting.' Invisibly, you may be giving yourself your own award to continue doing more.

Ultimately you are getting a sense of satisfaction and quiet mastery and an inner glow that no external incentive can give you.

Like the Gentle Rain

 All endings are also beginnings. It is just that we don't know it at the time. In the delightful book, *The Five People You Meet in Heaven*, Mitch Albom narrates the story of an 83-year-old war veteran discovering people who affected his life without anyone knowing about it.

This is true for managers also. Views from casual acquaintances who are not formally assigned the role of being a well-wisher can be extremely valuable. Their ideas come like gentle drops of rain that fall around you without making their presence felt too strongly, or being intrusive.

When I grew up in Calcutta (now Kolkata), it was a premier mercantile city, still maintaining the famous Boxwalla tradition. Any young person walking around the office areas like Fairlie Place and Brabourne Road would yearn for a management trainee job in those business firms—Andrew Yule, Balmer Lawrie, Bird and Company and Martin Burn—vanished, though hallowed, names from the silent nights of the past.

I was completing my final year BSc course and was a resident at the college hostel. Father de Bonhomme, the principal of St Xavier's College, asked me whether I would like to be recommended for a trainee job at Mackinnon Mackenzie. It was a fine firm, he could suggest only two from the whole college, and the salary would be ₹450 per month. I calmly said that I was honoured to be recommended, in reality, I was thrilled. I did not consult my father, who had by then moved to Bombay (now Mumbai).

With a borrowed suit and soaring dreams, I interviewed at the Mackinnon office. After being seen by two managers, I saw one Mohi Das, the managing director. He asked me several thoughtful questions. As I was getting convinced that I had done well and might get the job, he drew up close to me and asked, 'Son. May I call you that? Don't get me wrong, but you are just 18. You can have the job; we can train you quite well. But tell me, do you need the job? How is the family situation?'

I was a bit offended. What did my family situation have to do with the job? He clarified, 'Well, I have spent my career in one set of circumstances, but you will spend your career in an entirely different set of circumstances. I feel you should get a professional degree. You can always get this kind of job, son, unless the family situation requires you to get a job right now.'

How could he dangle one of the most prized jobs in front of me and then say what he had just said? I just did not want to listen to him. And I was quite clear about my future (or so I thought) without asking too many people!

Reluctantly, I decided after some further thought that I should mention to my father that I wish to accept the job. My father was furious that I could even think of taking a job. My dream job ended like a burst balloon. I went on to study further and joined Hindustan Lever subsequently.

I never met Mohi Das after that encounter. He retired in due course. A few years ago, I learned that he had died in

Coonoor. He would not remember this story even if I had the chance to remind him. He had influenced and counselled me about my career in a valuable way, but unknowingly.

Like gentle drops of fine rain that touch you but do not interfere with your life, casual advice comes your way. You need to listen to them and reflect on them, then take your own decision.

Particularly for a generation that is as blessed as young people are in today's India, this would be wise.

∽

A Zorba in Your Life

 An item that appears at the top of every manager's list of reasons for stress is the 'unfairness of the system'— poor feedback, inadequate career development, wrong promotions, etc. The challenge is not to wish away the so-called unfairness, but to learn how to cope with the stress sensibly. This requires a reflective mindset rather than an impulsive one. The story of Karan and Girdhar is instructive.

They were contenders for a top role, both were accomplished and had put in the years. When the time came, the board decided that Karan should be promoted. The dilemma was how to tell Girdhar. At a delicate meeting with Girdhar, the directors explained their difficulty in coming to a decision, but eventually they had decided in favour of Karan.

Girdhar's world crashed—the prized role he had worked for all his life was not to be his. His throat choked, tears almost welled out of his eyes and there was a storm of internal rage in his heart. 'After all the years I have devoted to this company,' he thought.

'Well, we have said what we have to,' continued the directors calmly, 'Please understand that it was difficult for us to make a choice. There could well be another opportunity for you in the future. So please do not think of leaving.'

Girdhar was livid internally. An instinct guided him to cope through reflection rather than act impulsively. He addressed the directors:

> 'During my career, I too have had to make choices about managers at levels below mine and have had to counsel the disappointed colleague. I have worked here because I felt this company was fair; I can not suddenly change that view. However, you can be fallible. In this case, I feel that you are making a big mistake. But you would expect me to feel so, hence I will not elaborate. You have made a choice as fairly as you could. I thank you for your advice to avoid haste. I will continue to work for some time, and I will think about my next course of action.'

That is what Girdhar did. He could deal with the issue calmly because he placed himself in the shoes of those who had to decide; he allowed himself the time to think things through.

He continued to work diligently but progressively became unhappy with the way things developed. Instead of cribbing, he found an alternative way to restore his happiness, i.e., a suitable opportunity elsewhere. He moved on to a new life. Very importantly, he retained warm ties with his old colleagues, and left with fond memories of the fun he had had working in that company.

We can feel fun only if we see fun in the work we do and the people we work with. Managers must learn to enjoy their work and career.

Author Morgan Scott Peck wrote, 'Life is a series of problems. Do you want to moan about them or solve them?' Managers, in fact everybody, seems to take their life and career far too seriously. They convince themselves about their crucial importance to their employer, almost to the point of being indispensable. Alas, graveyards are full of people who thought they were indispensable at some point in the past!

Managers must also learn to have fun because fun is a lightning rod for stress.

There was a fine film called *Zorba the Greek*, starring Anthony Quinn, a story about the relationship between two men. One was 'The Boss', who had looks, intelligence, health, money and education. He was a good person but all locked up inside. He did not enjoy life. He read and thought, but he did not know fun. Zorba was his assistant, fun-loving and taking each incident and day as it came.

Zorba told his boss, 'You have got everything, Boss, except one thing—madness. A man needs a little madness or he never cuts the rope and gets free.'

At the end of the film, Zorba taught the Boss to let go, to dance and laugh.

Managers need a Zorba in their careers and lives to serve as a lightning rod.

∾

The Mark of a Leader

 I touch upon an important border that every manager must cross—from being a functional manager to a leader of men. Many people underestimate this transition, often to their disadvantage.

You succeed as a functional manager by demonstrating superior knowledge, through using factors within your control to achieve ambitious goals and working pretty much through your own agenda. Very likely, you know more than your subordinates and can tell them what to do to solve a problem.

In a job 'across the border', you are working with people, who know more than you. You can do little by yourself; you depend on others to achieve targets.

You are a leader of men and facing the true test of a general manager.

Homi Khusrokhan had steadily risen within the finance and support functions of Glaxo, a large pharmaceuticals company. He had impeccable credentials as a UK qualified chartered accountant and as an alumnus of the London School of Economics. One day he was promoted as the general manager of a key business unit. He now bore responsibility for sales, marketing, purchasing and other functions.

The medical representatives (MR) of his organization were at a significant competitive advantage as compared to peer companies in the industry. MRs had nurtured the precious relationships with the profession and trade. Although the industry norm was that the MRs were members of an external union, it was not so in Glaxo at that time. It was important to keep it that way by being sensitive to their problems.

Homi's predecessors had come up from the field of or from the marketing department. He reckoned that the sales force would be apprehensive about having a finance person as their boss. He decided to meet the MRs and understand their problems. During his early meetings, he learned that the MRs had to perform demeaning and non-professional chores for their bosses. Autocracy, bordering on the indiscriminate use of power was rampant. To him, this was an issue of ethics! He was outraged.

Being of a calm and reflective nature, Homi decided not to react immediately and show his disapproval. As he worked his way through meetings with the area sales managers and regional sales managers, he found that a similar practice existed up the chain of command, right up to the general sales manager. He could hardly fire the whole team, nor could he antagonize every one of them by adopting an accusatory attitude.

In a private meeting with his top sales team, he shared his pain. In his 20 years, his bosses had never treated him that way, nor did he have such expectations from his subordinates. How could people not respect the dignity of others in the sales system? After a few meetings, it became clear that his method of helping them to see a different point of view was not working.

Worse still, his top colleagues said that this was actually a good way to manage; any softness would be damaging! They rationalized autocratic discipline as necessary to manage a dispersed group. Some experienced managers felt that the youngsters had to go through the mill as they themselves had.

Homi finally resorted to tackling his middle managers. He got them to debate the shared values that they would like to see in the company. When they did this, 'respect for people' featured strongly. Now it was easier for Homi to suggest, 'If that is the value you people want, let us go out and practise it uniformly!'

There followed a period of persistence and patience. The tough bit was giving marching orders to those that did not fall in line. Finally, the full team, including the senior sales managers, began to see Homi's point about 'respect for employees'. It took three years of hard work to dismantle the iniquitous system.

Homi's persistence and faith in relying on values had paid off. He worked through the problem and persuaded people rather than being moralistic or evangelical, or worse still, falling into the trap of ordering them to do as he felt.

You must lead your people, not as you were led earlier in your career, but as you would want to be led in the future. Homi advanced to assume leadership of the entire company. Later, he worked as a CEO-leader in Tata companies as well.

His reputation everywhere was of a person who led others in the same way that he liked to be led by his bosses.

∽

Managing the Inevitable Stress

One day, as a senior manager, I was contemplating issues of inter-departmental and inter-divisional working. All organizations seem to have similar problems in this respect, irrespective of the sector they operated in. This is understandable because the challenges of leadership remain the same and only the context changes. There is one unavoidable outcome. A career in any leadership position is stressful, for which future leaders must be prepared. Invariably, people look at the rewards and stature, without recognizing the mental and emotional load it comes with.

As a young engineer in production, at a factory working three shifts, the physical load on me was high. The pressure on outputs and meeting market demands was extraordinary. There could be no excuses for failure to meet shipment deadlines, whether the reasons were unanticipated absenteeism due to wedding season or breakdowns! The pressure to compensate for lost production and meeting all delivery deadlines on schedule persisted day after day. There was never a relaxed moment.

Sunday maintenance was essential to ensure that machines

were production-fit for the schedule. Since sizes, specs, brands, were all specific, doing better on some brands did not compensate for any failure to ship out market orders to specific destinations when they were required. Market estimates changed every 10 days; the production system, in turn, had to be fine-tuned and programmed to take care of peaking demands or sudden cancellations.

Mine was a 'bottleneck' department; there was very little float by way of spare machines. Breakdowns were, therefore, anathema. Yet, not sparing machines for scheduled maintenance would be short-sighted. One had to be an agile juggler with good stamina to cope with the ever-changing demands finely tuned to the market. When I spoke to my colleague in marketing, he explained that he was on the road 20 days of the month. He would be exhausted, covering remote corners of the country and eating haphazardly all the time. He spoke of customer reactions, quality complaints and products not reaching the markets on time or in the right quantities and losing out on opportunities as a consequence.

In later years, as the head of a department, I got an opportunity to see things from a slight distance, though still close to the pulse of the operation. Planning dynamically became critical. Interacting with materials/purchases became critical too, as their people informed me of uncertainties in procurement and the need to manage with alternative materials—which was often not to the liking of people in production, where consistency without surprises was preferred. Interaction with marketing became close too, with their personnel telling me of inevitable changes taking place causing a sudden spurt in demand which, obviously, could not be left for our competitors to meet.

Many Uncertainties

New brand launches consumed disproportionate attention as the uncertainties were high and everybody wanted to nurture a new star in the making. However, too much, too soon was as wasteful and bad as too little, too late.

Transport bottlenecks caused flutters in the system as there could be floods in some parts of the country and transit times were longer via alternative routes. Road permits and forms for interstate movement caused irritating bottlenecks. A small change in specifications, based on market feedback, caused major upheavals in production scheduling—old stocks had to be flushed out of markets and new stocks moved in almost seamlessly, so that customer demands were always fulfilled without glitches. The pressure to constantly cope with changes was both physical and mental. If a problem in industrial relations rocked the boat, then uncertainties only increased, and one had to grapple with an additional variable at an inconvenient time, even whilst grasping quality impacts that may happen during such volatile times, until matters settled down. Improving communications between interacting functions became critical. Everyone had their complaints. As a divisional CEO of a strategic business unit, the pressures multiplied across several units and functions, with the additional responsibility for bringing in new business and ensuring that committed profits were delivered as per business plans. The entire gamut of managing across functions (Finance-Purchasing-Marketing-Production-Engineering-MIS-Legal-Personnel) became a primary responsibility even though my familiarity with each of these functions was not at the same level. One had to acquire an appreciation of other functions even while getting everyone to cooperate across functional boundaries for the overall purpose of profit, growth and survival.

Business strategy and competitiveness came strongly into the fray. The emotional toll by way of anxiety and uncertainty was higher as the buck stopped with me and a single person had to be held responsible for the bottom line. Issues of audit, safety and sustainability could not be taken lightly. They had to be dealt with, along with aspects of governance in the division. These have evolved greatly from the days since the time one joined an organization fresh.

The above examples should give the reader a glimpse of the physical, mental and emotional pressures that are inevitable in any position of leadership. The proportion of each may vary with positions in the hierarchy. A new IT system during its launch can create extraordinary demands on all managers at the time of 'going live'. A new technology introduced, like a new paper machine, will make demands up and down the system and across functions, causing stress until everything connected with it gradually settles down.

Now, moving up the hierarchy, an executive director responsible for several businesses or functions across businesses cannot rely upon his past track record alone. He must be abreast of issues of corporate governance, secretarial functions, share responsibilities, environmental responsibilities and sustainability and the role of the media. Understanding the roles of the many non-executive directors requires time and effort and cannot be viewed as unfamiliar people asking pesky questions without knowing the nuts and bolts of the company's businesses.

The nature of corporate governance has evolved, especially from the days of Enron in 2001, into more transparent reporting and disclosures, and the need for balancing executive power with checks and balances by the non-executive directors. The Board committees are now mandatory as per Securities and Exchange Board of India (SEBI)—especially the Audit Committee, the Nominations & Remuneration Committee, the Investors Committee, the Independent Directors Committee and the methodology to deal with whistleblower complaints. In addition, there is the Corporate Social Responsibility (CSR) committee as well.

Does all of this create stress? It does produce mental and emotional stress—most often because of the way people think and interact, and this is the principal theme of this book.

The Bhopal gas tragedy of 1984 or the Exxon Valdez oil spill of 1989 or Enron scandal of 2000–1 threw managing directors into a tizzy in the glare of media and legal complications that they had never envisaged before. Volkswagen and its software designed to understate diesel fuel emissions took the media by storm. Carlos Ghosn's compensation tore apart Renault–Nissan into a France versus Japan debate.

Chairman and CEO

The role of the chairman remains a complex one. Many American corporations prefer an executive chairman. However, world opinion has veered around to splitting the office of the chairman—a non-executive chairman who leads the Board of Directors on governance and ensures the participation of all members at Board meetings, and a CEO/managing director who runs the company. This is a complex arrangement. Invariably, the non-executive directors, other than those representing institutional shareholders, are appointed with the consent of the CEO and may feel a sense of obligation to them.

The Companies Act does not allow independent directors to stay on for more than two consecutive terms of five years each—distinct from the past when they have served for 20-year stretches. How and where does the Board draw a line between allowing unfettered freedom and reining in the CEO with checks and balances? The recent issues concerning ICICI and Infosys are cases in point.

Is debate and dissent encouraged in Board meetings? Can nomination committees debate CEO succession in a free manner or can non-executive directors debate this at the independent directors meeting allowed at least once a year? Do they have enough exposure to gauge the management talent two or three levels down from the Board of Directors?

The stress caused by such weighty matters can be quite different from the more routine experiences of physical, mental and emotional stress. Issues of strategy are often left to the executive directors and the CEO, but the Board of Directors needs to apply its mind and not allow the company to go belly up in a crisis, as has happened with Satyam, Kingfisher, IL&FS and Jet Airways. In all these cases, better corporate governance could have saved these companies long before they hit a crisis of unmanageable proportions.

The CEO often realizes that, suddenly, time is no longer his. People keep telling him he is all powerful, but it does not feel like that! Time and effort are spent in dealing with Board matters, shareholder matters, investors, media and the government. This is stress of another kind, almost unrelated to the daily activities of his company.

His confidence in knowing his company and its businesses does not seem as relevant anymore. Anything that he says gets (mis)interpreted. If he keeps quiet, that is given an interpretation too! People are often telling him what they think he'd like to hear. Real news is frequently masked or kept away from him. At times he feels badly cut off and lonely.

There is a time lag in decisions taking effect, and that can be difficult. If he steps on the accelerator, that runs the danger of becoming the norm. If he expresses an opinion too strongly, it short-circuits all other communication in the system. If he encourages opinions to be expressed around the table, people feel he is becoming too democratic or is avoiding taking decisions on his own. Sometimes he feels all decision-making is being delegated upwards. Whoever said that the CEO has reached the top and is free of stress, didn't know what they were talking about!

✍

The Happiness Code

Nobody can help an individual who has decided to be unhappy. Conversely nobody is required to help an intrinsically happy person.

Every individual has his or her happiness neatly packed into a locker. The locker can be opened using a secret code number. The code number to the lock is known to only one person, which is that individual, who alone can open the lock to be happy, or keep it locked and remain unhappy. The secret code number is unique and cannot be shared with anyone else, be it a sibling, a spouse or a dear friend. If a person has chosen to be happy, nobody can stop him (or her). Conversely, if the person has chosen to be unhappy, no other individual can help that person. This is a universal reality.

All human beings increasingly struggle with the stress of life, trying to understand and achieve what success in career and life means, realizing that the accomplishment of such success does not automatically lead to contentment and fulfilment and figuring out how to judge events and situations without judging people. The important lesson most people learn is that there is no universally acceptable measure of what success is. Success depends on how the individual views his or her goals in life and how he or she thinks meaning can be found in career and life.

Understanding this reality makes success and the lenses through which to view life goals and accomplishments rather ambiguous, personal and quite wide open. And yet all the billions of people on this planet are chasing success as though it is a reality—a tangible, palpable reality.

I have explored the nuances that lightly surround perceptions of success and fulfilment and also, tried to appreciate the relationship of success with one's views about feeling fulfilled. Career and life books sometimes come through as offering cookie-cutter tips to avid readers who want instant, pre-packaged wisdom. They pretend to suggest action rather than inspire thinking. That is why there are several popular books on techniques, littered with the mundane and the mechanical. Frankly, if it were that easy, everybody would be successful and fulfilled. There can be no definitive book of rules and tips about success and fulfilment.

The life stories of celebrities are highly readable and inspirational. Celebrities are written about a lot, and their stories are commented upon a lot, some aspects about them also suffer exaggeration and distortion. The stories of celebrities do bear interest for the reader because those stories are about people widely accepted to be successful. Their stories are presented like fairy tales that romanticize rather than depict stark realities.

You learn more from PLU—people like us. PLU inspire as well as instruct readers in different ways as compared to celebrity tales. It is comforting for ordinary people to know that PLU, also struggle to think through dilemmas, do not know precisely what they want out of their lives and careers or struggle to live a life of fulfilment despite possessing all the trappings of success.

PLU are unable to recall the time when they had a eureka moment. Interesting ideas are clicking in their brain often, but it is not recognized by them as eureka moments and there is no thunder and lightning that blinds their mind! Why should the reader be interested in the lives of PLU, ordinary characters?

As human beings, like the reader, the PLU have three life influences: first, their genetic personality; second, their inner journey of experiences (self-awareness, mental complexity, childhood character influences); third, their outer influences (education, parents, job and friends). These merge into one track to influence how they think and act. This integrated track defines who they are as human beings. So when you read about other people or interact with friends and work colleagues, if you wish to understand that person as an integrated human being, as you should be, then you need to understand that person's inner and outer life influences.

When a child is born, it can be likened to a smooth pebble of a certain size and colour. As the child grows, throughout its life, experiences leave an impact on the smooth pebble—chips, marks and incisions—so that each pebble develops a unique contour of its own.

A France-based American writer, Pamela Druckerman, expressed an imaginative view by suggesting that each person has a shape that must fit into the jigsaw of the world. 'Somewhere in the world, there is a gap shaped just like you. Once you find it, you will slide right in.' Said in French, it reads, *vous allez trouver votre place.*

To illustrate the point about finding a gap that is shaped just like you, I recall the story of Leela Chitnis, India's leading film star of the 1940s, who found the gap shaped like her[1].

Leela was the skinny and gawky daughter of a professor and she wore thick glasses. She fell in love with an urbane gentleman who was 14 years her senior, Gajanand Chitnis, who was involved with the Marathi stage as a writer and director of plays. Gajanand Chitnis was not economically successful, so the shy and self-conscious Leela started accompanying her husband to rehearsals and earned a bit by helping with the costumes and the sets.

Every evening she watched and observed the goings-on; something must have been churning in her brain. One day, the heroine of the play failed to turn up. Leela was thrust on the stage only because she had attended the endless rehearsals. She felt hugely challenged, but she performed with a natural élan and did brilliantly. Very soon, offers for roles poured in and she signed her first film.

Until 1940, Lux soap was always advertised with foreign film stars because Indians considered it of low character to model for advertisements. In 1940, when Lux sought Indian models, Leela was the first to be chosen. Soon thereafter, she became a leading Hindi film star. In her quest for a gap she could fit into, she viewed events and things differently from other people.

As Leela's story of apparent coincidences demonstrates, she found the gap that was shaped like her.

Differing Views of the World

When we see world maps, we are used to seeing the Americas on the left side and Europe and Africa approximately in the

---

[1]'My Aunt Leela', *The Indian Express*, 9 October 2005, https://indianexpress.com/article/news-archive/my-aunt-leela/.

middle. New Zealand appears in the bottom far-right corner. When I visited New Zealand, I found an interesting, almost unrecognizable version of a world map, constructed from New Zealand's perspective.

New Zealand was right in the upper middle of the map. The mass of Europe, Asia and Africa spread from below, upwards on the right side, like a mushroom. The Americas appeared on the left, but with the United States and Canada below Brazil. Argentina was above Brazil and was sticking upwards. They had merely turned the map upside down and placed New Zealand at the centre. The map presented the reality through a different lens[2]. The image of this New Zealand-centred world map makes a subtle point about what we remember of what we see.

We lead our lives in concentric circles. In the first circle, there is a big 'I'. The nuclear family appears large and close. In the second circle appear childhood friends, school friends, as well as relatives. In the third circle, we accommodate college friends, work acquaintances and relationships. In the fourth circle, there are casual friends and easy-to-forget relationships and episodes. In such a map of concentric circles, the deeply impactful people for you, whether positively or negatively, appear to be large and the others less so.

The brain stores memories of people and events differently for different people even though those people witness or experience the same event. This multiplicity is captured brilliantly in the 1950 Japanese film, *Rashomon*, directed by Akira Kurosawa. A woodcutter and a priest are sitting together under a shelter, trying to stay dry from the heavy downpour of rain. A commoner joins, thus making a threesome, and they

---

[2]www.flourish.org/upsidedownmap/

discuss the brutal murder of a samurai warrior by a bandit in the forest a little while ago. There are multiple versions of what actually transpired, by the priest, the woodcutter, the bandit and the samurai's wife. The gripping plot of the film involves these characters providing alternative, self-serving and contradictory versions of the same incident.

A memoir is what the author remembers. A memoir is telling a truth as the writer sees it. One memoir writer discovered that her account of the first meeting with her ex-boyfriend was completely different from his. Such situations arise because there are multiple perspectives involved in the viewing of a certain event or even relationship.

Learning from my own experiences and after giving it much thought, I can say:

1. Your 'shape' is determined by the way you view events and people in the world around you.
2. When you find and fit into the gap that has a 'shape' like you, you feel successful and fulfilled.

Societies everywhere have found that ideas and life lessons are best communicated through anecdotes, parables and epics. Stories have proved durable and effective for centuries in civilizations all over the world. The revival of mythological themes in the Indian publishing industry in recent years is further evidence of the power of such storytelling, of the value of conversing with the heart rather than only with the head.

Everybody struggles to reconcile many aspects of work and family life. Questions such as:

♦ How can you reconcile differing views of the same person?
♦ How can a person get the best out of both, their career and relationships?

◆ Are there fixed features of a good character and a good life?

◆ Can character be consistent under all circumstances?

◆ How can one be inspired by others' leadership while accepting their faults?

◆ Is our perception of others based on whether their virtues are emphasized or their failings?

◆ How can one reconcile others' virtues and failings simultaneously?

◆ Do external events constitute a balanced and fulfilling life or an internal mindset?

I think humans are born to learn, not to be taught. To illustrate this point about human beings being born to learn, not taught, I recall the story of B.K. Nehru, a scion of the Nehru family which has been a leading family in Indian governance since the Independence.

B.K. Nehru was conversing with his London School of Economics professor Harold Laski some 15 years after his graduation. A bit hesitatingly, Nehru told his professor that he had found little use of the professor's teachings during his career in the Indian Civil Service. The deep-thinking Laski responded, 'That is quite okay. I was not trying to teach you lessons in economics, I was merely teaching you how to think. And that I seem to have done very well, from what you say.'

I found that writing life experiences as instructive and, perhaps, inspiring stories is not challenging to me alone. Is it not more valuable if experienced people who have learnt from their life experiences write about the dilemmas they faced? Books shouldn't be only about rich and famous people, they should also include ordinary people—the kind of people one encounters during their career and life. This is why we wrote this book.

It appears that you can write your way to happiness. Scientific studies have revealed that writing about oneself and personal experiences can be beneficial to health. We all have a personal narrative that shapes our view of the world and ourselves. By writing and then editing our own stories, we can change our perception of ourselves and identify obstacles that stand in the way of our well-being.

As psychologist Brené Brown stated in her much-viewed TED talk, that it is perhaps best to confront one's vulnerabilities.[3] It may be the best way to deal with that enervating sense of vulnerability if it is standing between expressing oneself fully and keeping quiet. I decided to confront my vulnerability about whether my narrative will be interesting to the anonymous reader out there.

∽

---

[3]Brené Brown, 'The Power of Vulnerability', TEDxHouston, June 2010, https://www.ted.com/talks/brene_brown_the_power_of_vulnerability?language=en.

Cultivate the Right Fear

Events in faraway Chennai showed how an episode like 9/11 could have a destructive influence on people, even when they are far removed from the situation. That misguided youth could be goaded into seeing the terrorist attack as a revolt against authority, was unthinkable.

The ITC management had been in negotiations with the union at its Tiruvottiyur, Chennai factory. I was the head of the business division at that time. A few meetings had taken place at the office of the Joint Commissioner of Labour. There was a good offer on the table but a full acceptance on all points had not yet been reached for a long term agreement.

Warning signs of dissatisfaction had appeared on the horizon a year ago, when a new guard had been elected. The new union leaders had adopted a militant posture, perhaps encouraged by extraneous local developments in the neighbourhood where a Personnel Manager had been stabbed. The doors of collective bargaining were kept open and negotiations started.

In October of 2001, news came in that there had been a wildcat strike by the young office-bearers of the Union. ITC managers had been attacked and new equipment damaged. A group of managers and secretaries in the factory general office had been *gheraoed* and threatened with death, or were even being burned alive. Wounded managers were somehow moved to the hospital. The local police were alerted and with their help, the gherao was lifted by late evening. The Union president came into the factory and addressed the workmen and asked them to disperse, go home and await further instructions, as they were on a strike.

About 15 managers had suffered bruises, cuts and direct blows. A stocktaking was carried out as to how events unfolded that fateful afternoon in the late shift. Notices were put up at the factory gate, stating that an unprecedented lightning strike had occurred, accompanied by widespread violence against staff and machinery, even while an offer was on the table and negotiations were at an advanced stage in the presence of the Joint Commissioner of Labour.

The factory was kept open for work.

Nobody reported for work during the night shift or the following morning or for the next few weeks. Reports were filed with the Labour Department, on the violence and the continuation of the lightning strike. A letter was also addressed to the Union president. A brief notice was published in the newspapers, narrating the unfortunate events, despite the factory being kept open for work and an offer being under discussion mediated by the Labour Department. Chargesheets based on eyewitness accounts were posted to errant workmen and simultaneously displayed on the main noticeboard and the gate for communication of dates of the inquiry.

Meanwhile, the head office of ITC Ltd in Kolkata had many questions about whether the local management had been too tough and whether there had been adequate caution in not allowing the collective bargaining process to go out of control.

As a Corporate Management Committee member, I took the stand with head office that the factory manager, the CEO and his team should be fully supported and that we should not make impulsive changes. The task of rehabilitation was of prime importance. Damaged machinery had to be repaired with insurance claims filed, and peace and order and confidence had to be restored in the workplace. Continuity had to be ensured for customers. Further the principle of 'no work, no pay' had to be upheld and action taken on indiscipline after giving fair opportunities for defence through inquiries. Chargesheets had already been sent to the errant workmen. The lawyers of the Union, along with the Union president, were advised too. Key officials of the government were met and kept apprised of the full details, including photographs of the incident.

Within two months, workmen started reporting voluntarily to work in phases after signing an undertaking of good behaviour and commitment to abide by the factory's rules and regulations. Machinery was repaired and put back in operation—although some took longer, considering the damage done to them. In a matter of six months, operations were back to normal with a heightened sense of enthusiasm to meet customer orders. Simultaneously, actions including dismissals were carried out after due process.

It seemed to be a miracle that the same factory was achieving new heights of productivity and quality and making good profits too. The factory was getting ready for a fresh investment, determined to set aside the past and build the future. Managers and workmen seemed imbued with a new sense of energy of doing things right to succeed with a shared objective of growth.

The long-term agreement had still not been signed; it remained pending as it was not clear as to whom to negotiate with. A thought emerged that direct talks with the workmen in batches could be made to succeed and that it would be more transparent than any method they had used so far. The thought seemed to catch on after some initial hesitation and then spread with smiles all around. Collective bargaining picked up momentum again.

A long-term agreement was signed for five years with all 400 plus workmen, individually and collectively representing themselves and the Union. It was implemented fully and smoothly even as it was being signed. This was another first in ITC's history, despite the difficult circumstances that preceded it. The democratic framework imposed greater responsibility on managers to coordinate better and communicate clearly and transparently and to answer questions patiently. The factory manager, R. Senguttuvan, demonstrated excellent communication and leadership skills during the crisis and right through the signing of a historic long-term agreement. He was supported by the CEO, G.M.K. Raju.

Senguttuvan became the chief operating officer and then subsequently the CEO of the Packaging & Printing Division, taking it from strength to strength.

Open and Sensitive Communication

Productivity, morale and business performance went up steadily and consistently. Three more rounds on similar agreements took place peacefully and constructively till 2019. The sceptics have watched this process unfold and have been surprised at the win-win climate created. Many other milestones were achieved in the journey forward, setting new standards of safety and quality.

The Tiruvottiyur factory won the British Safety Council

Sword of Honour and got a Level 8 International Quality Rating System of DNV (IQRS). It had been the highest quality standard at that time and Tiruvottiyur became the first of ITC's factories to go additionally environmentally green with 100 per cent wind energy.

It implemented the SAP software in record time. It would rank as one of the most modern packaging factories in the world, with productivity benchmarked to standards in the USA, Europe and Japan. It remains a nimble exporter with a track record of fulfilling export obligations ahead of time for machinery imported at zero duty.

The above events establish the benefits of a firm and level-headed approach of doing things properly. This will pay off dividends in the long run. Management can devise principles of being fair and sincere and approachable even while pursuing business goals in a competitive context.

In a small way, the Tiruvottiyur example is an expression of the same resurgent spirit in ITC. Credit must go to the entire teams of managers and workmen who focused on doing things properly to rebuild everything despite a violent and discouraging setback. This is positive and constructive energy at work.

The incident drove home the lesson that you should not fear losing, but you should fear not doing things properly.

∞

The Power of Humility

 I joined HLL as a computer analyst after an engineering degree. I suffered from a common trait that many young people show—I had quite a lofty idea about technology, matched by a quiet and unexpressed disdain for functions such as selling and accounting. It was cerebral work that I had to do in the early years. I did it on my own and the challenge was of a personal and analytical nature. With the passage of time and aspirations for career progress, my ideas changed.

In the fifth year, I chose to move to an operational role in the sales function. The general sales manager was Bhau Phansalkar, who insisted that I should train all over again as a van salesman. He felt that I should aim to demonstrate my ability to lead a team of market salesmen who were twice my age. I was quite miffed. What kind of challenge was this? Was I not smart enough to do all that and more? I did not appreciate being subjected to this 'hardship.' Many years later, I realized the significance.

Getting superior work done by frontline colleagues, motivating them, not talking down to them, securing their commitment to your goals—all these may appear simple. But they are the muscle of a management role and the only way to learn them is by doing them. One also realizes the complexity of human emotions and the need to take a genuine interest in people, not just talk about it. I did retrain as a van salesman and learnt all those things that I had mistakenly assumed were easy enough.

About eight years into my job, a development occurred that I regard as a career bend. I was the branch sales manager in western India and my boss was a warm but tough taskmaster called Ranjit Talwar. In those days, production capacities were controlled, and products used to be in short supply due to the licence regime in the country. A key task of sales managers was to serve consumers by achieving wide and equitable distribution of these short supply products—put simply, the task was to spread the shortage widely to minimize inconvenience to consumers.

A complaint was received that our cooking product, Dalda, was being marketed for a higher than permitted price by one of our two Pune distributors. Talwar assigned me the responsibility to investigate and recommend a course of action. I was aware that such investigations rarely produced conclusive, ironclad evidence. Even if the allegations were true, there could only be a strongly suggestive or near conclusive proof at best. I was aware that a fair decision on such a matter would send an important message to other distributors about the company's widely proclaimed commitment to an honest distribution system.

Thus, in such cases, it is difficult to establish incontrovertible proof one way or the other. One has to view the facts within a context of events. As it so happened, after my field work, I concluded that the distributor had indeed marketed the product at an unfair price. Further, the punishment was clear to me: his distributorship had to be terminated. But there was a major problem.

The accused had been a loyal soap distributor of the company for 35 years. The distributor had been associated with the firm for over two generation as it had originally been with his father. He knew all the senior managers extremely well, including Ranjit Talwar and Bhau Phansalkar. And here I was, all of 29, recommending the termination of a distributorship older than I was! I was warned by colleagues that I could face severe questioning and pressure from my seniors. Some even advised taking a 'more pragmatic' stand.

I felt scared and uncertain.

I was interviewed and asked many questions by Talwar and Phansalkar, and even the company's legal director, Shamdas Gursahani. I guess I must have sounded convincing without seeming rigid. To the credit of the seniors in the company, with a great deal of anguish, HLL did terminate the distributorship. Contrary to the predictions of politics and pressure, it was a professional process. But I did not know that it would be so, and felt that I was taking a big risk.

The distributor found his case weak on the real ground of investigation, so he escalated the matter as an issue of the company practising territorial restrictions on sales and restrictive trade practices to the detriment of the consumer. This spiralled into a case at the Monopolies and Restrictive Trade Practices (MRTP) Commission.

For me, this was a huge personal development and learning. In hindsight, I learnt that it is not only the functional competencies one needs to master, but also the perseverance to stand firm with certain principles and standards, whatever be the threats or consequences.

Accept a Mistake

Another incident occurred later in my career. On a hot, sweltering June day in the twentieth year of service, Chairman Ashok Ganguly called me and expressed the company's satisfaction with my work and invited me to join the company's management committee as the exports director. I was 41, not expecting the promotion at the time and was understandably over the moon. However, my elation was short-lived.

Three months later, disaster struck. The company had been exporting merchandise that was unfamiliar to its core business in household products, so we had recruited some specialist managers from these trades to bring in domain knowledge. We had people with expertise in items as diverse as woollen carpets, leather and garments. It was quite a challenge to induct these new recruits into the company's culture, particularly the scrupulously honest practices and professionalism. These were not the hallmarks of the small operators who dominated such fields.

A smart manager called Muktesh Pant used to work as my deputy at that time in HLL Exports. Muktesh and I stumbled on the fact that one such specialist manager had swindled the company of ₹1 crore, which was a lot of money in 1987, even for HLL. The evidence was indicative, but not solid. What was I to do?

I went to my long-time mentor, a director called Bipin Shah. He urged me to inform the chairman immediately. Thereafter, the course of action would be devised by the company rather than my department. It seems obvious, once stated, but it is not what most people would naturally want to do. The natural response would be to try and fix the problem. If avoidable, why involve others? I was very, very anxious.

What would people think of me, a new director with a fraud on his hands? Were my facts right? Had I alarmed everybody prematurely? I was in a quandary. But Bipin Shah had always advised me well, so I gathered courage and knocked on the chairman's door.

Ashok Ganguly was a warm as well as tough manager, a combination that could leave the bearer of bad tidings in a bit of confusion. Which face would I see? My throat was dry as I told him about what I had to. He raised his eyebrows sharply and looked at me with palpable shock on his face. As I was getting ready for a screaming, he suddenly seemed to soften. 'Gopal, sit down, have a glass of water,' he said. 'Now tell me again, what else do you know so far?'

It was a magical moment, because from perceiving him as a potential tormentor and judge, I saw him as an ally. Instead of being my problem, he suddenly seemed to become my possible solution. I learned that if a boss could support his subordinate when the latter has hit big trouble, surely there is a huge leadership lesson in it.

Over the next 12 months, the top management of the company's finance and legal departments helped me and Muktesh Pant unravel the mess, take corrective action and bring this sordid matter to an end. Regrettably, the company never got back the ₹1 crore. It became my greatest lesson in humility.

∞

Unilever globally acquired Lipton through a deal in the early 1970s. In India, Lipton was a serious competitor to Brooke Bond in the branded-tea market, with a share of about half of Brooke Bond's. For several reasons, Lipton India had become a problem company for Unilever by the early 1980s.

My old boss, Bipin Shah, was specially selected to go into this troubled company to fix its problems. Bipin was a consummate turnaround artist with very fine commercial sense and a terrific intuition for business. But the challenges he faced were considerable. Even while he was at work, in a global deal in the mid-1980s, Brooke Bond was globally acquired by Unilever.

So, now suddenly, Brooke Bond India and Lipton India were the progeny of the same parent! However, Brooke Bond India continued to make life difficult for Lipton India because the companies were run on a stand-alone basis at an arm's length. So, this is the story of two fierce rivals for over 60 years, who suddenly found themselves as sons of the same parent due to some global moves.

Lipton's market share was stagnant, its cost structure was bloated, it was a single-product (tea) company, its cash generation was stressed; Brooke Bond India was not making Lipton's life easy in the marketplace. Brooke Bond India had twice the volume of Lipton, had healthy cash generation and commanded the market.

In the early '80s, a Unilever director, T. Thomas, decided to call on C.S. Samuel, the chairman of Brooke Bond India. He had an agenda born out of humility, that is, to assess the probability of survival of Lipton—selling out must have been a distinct option from Unilever's perspective. Such a conversation would not normally have been easy, but in this case, it became possible because Thomas and Samuel had worked together at Hindustan Lever in the 1960s. Thomas had been a technical manager and Samuel an accountant.

Thomas and Samuel separately recounted this meeting to me several years later, and both recalled identical versions of what transpired. Samuel understood the predicament of Lipton, which was candidly outlined by Thomas. After all, his company was partly responsible for some of the woes of Lipton, though some other woes were, in his opinion, self-inflicted. He could not help in any meaningful way, Samuel asserted.

But for sure, Unilever should dismiss the option of selling out its stake in Lipton. 'For its own long-term interest, Brooke Bond needs Lipton India to be a strong competitor, so Unilever should invest in seeing how to strengthen Lipton,' he commented. A rather strange attitude, one might have thought, because one can imagine CEO Samuel doing a delighted jig at the misery of his main competitor.

But Samuel had realized that the complete removal of Lipton India would stultify Brooke Bond India into complacence. So, he took a long-term view, enlightened self-interest no doubt, but nonetheless far-sighted.

Lipton India survived and grew, so did Brooke Bond India. Finally, in 1994–95, Lipton India was merged with Brooke Bond India. One year later, I returned to India to lead the merged company. Tea volumes and margins were under great pressure, partly due to a downturn in the tea industry, but also due to the emotional mayhem that accompanies such mergers. The most common comment I heard from managers was that in the absence of any competitive threat, the new company had nobody to fight with. I could not possibly encourage such a discussion, as the merger was by then a *fait accompli*; life had to go on.

Meanwhile, Tata Tea was emerging and by the early '90s, Tata Tea began to pose some challenge to the two dominant branded tea players, Lipton and Brooke Bond! I will always wonder what might have happened if Lipton and Brooke Bond had not merged in 1993!

∽

UNDERSTANDING OTHERS

Emotion-laced Facts Work

Several years ago, I became aware of *The Parable of the Sadhu,* published in the Harvard Business Review. Bowen McCoy was a participant in a sabbatical for company executives. He walked through villages in the Himalayas and climbed many mountains. One of his experiences was in Nepal.

He and the other mountaineers were bound for the holy city of Muktinath through a challenging 18,000-feet pass. After resting at 15,500 feet, the team set out for the final assault. Just then, they found a sadhu, lying in the snow and still alive. He was near naked and barefoot, shivering and suffering from hypothermia. He was probably on the return journey after visiting the shrines at Muktinath; it was unclear how and why he had reached the delicate life-and-death condition he was found in.

They assigned some tasks to each other. As a result, the sadhu was transported a few hundred feet down and left there, in the hope that someone would find him. The question was: what else should the mountaineers have done? Was what they did ethical? Was there a difference between individual and corporate ethics?

This was discussed energetically during an HBS Advanced Management Programme. Some Western managers opined that the action of the mountaineers was not ethical; others thought that their action was practical but still not ethical. The Indian in the group questioned whether it was at all a question of ethics.

She said, 'Every morning as I drive in Bombay, I see people who are poor, in frail health and suffering from disability or disease. The humanity in me says I should stop to help them, my pragmatism points out that, in that case, I would never be able to stray more than half a mile from my house. Unfortunately, there is a lot of misery even as India changes. If it becomes an ethical question, no Indian can be at peace with his conscience.'

There was a stunned silence. A very emotional discussion followed. There were no answers, but the discussion threw up questions to reflect upon. Above all, emotion made the session a 'story', and not another 'incident'.

Rational case studies are easily forgotten, but the participants would never forget the parable of the sadhu!

The connection between emotion and recall is exemplified by the work of two professors at Irvine, California. Two groups were told the same story, but in very different ways. One group was just presented with the facts, in an unexciting and sequential manner. For the other group, the content and the style was emotion heavy. After several weeks, both groups were tested for recall. The emotion-laden group could recall the sequence far more vividly although not necessarily, more accurately. The professors called this 'flashbulb memory'.

Another example is Gabriel Garcia Marquez's novella, *Chronicle of a Death Foretold*. It is about a man who returned to the village where a violent murder had occurred several years ago. The villagers recalled the episode in a matter-of-fact way. However, the relations and close friends of the murdered man remembered things which the villagers did not. The family's memory was not necessarily accurate, but it brought the episode to life vividly.

Simple idea, supported by a simple story, could be a positive format for learning and reflection and practising managers could find that useful.

After all, management is not rocket science, you don't need deep and technical know-how. It is all about people and emotions, accompanied by some essential intelligence and training.

As you think about your business life, you will recognize several incidents and stories that have shaped you. 'Incident' refers to a *factual* recollection of what happened. 'Story' refers to an *emotional* memory of what you felt. They are very different, and so is their influence.

Managers are trained to be rational and to shun emotion. This may not always be the best approach.

∽

 Dr Atul Gawande, the famous doctor who wrote *The Checklist Manifesto*, has advocated the enormous value of simple checklists in improving success rates. He shares examples not only from hospitals and medical care but from a host of diverse applications.

This is logical and sensible and appeals to the head. If that is the case, why is it so difficult to practise? I discussed this issue with a few friends and got thought-provoking responses:

Ajay: Dr Gawande presents it very well and his style is so appealing. But it is tough to put into practice beyond a day.

Shyam: I made an enthusiastic start and got it going for a few weeks. It is impossible to get others to appreciate what needs to be done. They read the book and say it is very good. Then nothing happens!

Sridhar: You know, every now and then, somebody writes a book based on their experience. It is like a novel that you read in one sitting and enjoy until you put the book down and forget about it for a couple of years until the context comes back a little differently. Then it seems too late.

(This came to me as a valid reminder as my co-author and I write this book!)

I recall a friend of mine telling me how he clutched his chest in pain as he got off the aircraft that summer morning on an early flight to Delhi. He said he collapsed and felt drained. The airline staff rushed to his rescue. An ambulance was called and he was taken to a nearby hospital and wheeled into emergency. In the haze of the events that followed, the doctor told him he had had a heart attack and had three blocks. Stents needed to be put in right away. He retrieved a medical insurance number and his wife's telephone number. He did not remember the exact sequence thereafter, but he was successfully operated on and woke up to see his wife standing next to him, looking at him with serious concern. He managed to smile and she smiled back in relief.

Family members and friends came to see him and wish him a speedy recovery. Everybody said he was lucky to have received timely help after landing in Delhi. Some said he had been pushing himself too hard on his travel schedules. A few suggested that a change in lifestyle and leaner eating habits are in order. The doctors advised an exercise regimen and regular walking after discharge from the hospital. He improved steadily and was back at work soon. The emergency had passed.

Emotional Impact

I stopped to pause and reflect at how his overwhelming confidence had changed to cautious optimism with one incident. Then I thought again about *The Checklist Manifesto*. The narration by my friend in everyday language about his experience in Delhi was more impactful. Naturally, our personal association had made a difference. His telling me about a real life-changing experience made another big difference. I could relate to everything he said. I even conjectured what might have happened had I been in his shoes that summer morning and had it happened to me! Did I need to get a medical check-up done, one that I had been postponing due to other priorities? Were my eating and lifestyle habits alright or was I pushing my luck until something happened to me, like my friend?

It seemed to fall into place somewhat as follows:

- Facts speak to the head
- Emotions speak to the heart
- Facts and emotions put together as a narrative make an impact; they are remembered as stories

The tradition of grandparents telling children stories makes for a great example. These stories, conveyed with vivid gestures and changes of voice and tone, from a trusted and affectionate source, stay with you for a lifetime. Like with a tape, your memory can be rewound and played easily at short notice.

How do organizations deal with formal and organizational communications, especially to transfer learnings? There are times when facts are urgently needed; questions to be answered with figures. There are other times when a narrative is appropriate enough to communicate.

Experiences and emotions must be woven into a story that paints the bigger picture, which is not obvious at the time of each incident. Such stories can be communicated for fast recall. Tools and checklists and training will still be required to complete the tasks. The exercise becomes more challenging if the likelihood of the incidents occurring is low and the context is far removed from the listener's everyday experiences or seems too abstract.

First person narratives of experience have all the ingredients of good stories. There is a human being talking to another and this always blends facts with emotions. The perceptions associated with such emotions become the quick reference tags for future recall.

A narrative can bring back lessons and memories of *The Longest Day*, a film that endeavours to capture the D-Day landings into a story. Here is an example:

> A soldier explains where he was on D-Day on 6 June 1944 and how menacing the tides were on Omaha beach as some of the floating tanks sank right to the bottom of the sea with their full crews. He recalls his fears as he stumbled onto Omaha beach under a fusillade of gunfire. He was determined to achieve his goal for Day One. He was talking rapidly with his companion who abruptly fell silent. He turned, shocked to see his companion lying flat on his back with a nasty hole in his head. There was no time to cry as others screamed at him to keep running; his heavy backpack seemed to get heavier with every

step. The light was faint; it was the crack of dawn. He felt something hot and sticky on his arm—was it his own blood? There was no time to think or worry as he moved ahead.

In cold prose, this scenario could have happened at other beaches too. Somebody at the American Staff College quickly put together the learnings for the use of frontline training for the Pacific. Were the backpacks too heavy as soldiers waded through waist-deep water and gunfire? Could an IV tube be attached to the helmet for quick relief? Were the floating tanks released too early at Omaha?

The challenge of passing on one's learnings is daunting. Even the most routine tasks have challenges when it comes to communicating to a listener how to ensure 100 per cent success, 100 per cent of the time. It seems simple with a tried and tested checklist but remains elusive in practice, especially where groups are involved.

Most people want to get it right, maybe 90 per cent true, 90 per cent of the time. Yet in a series of interdependent tasks, if each performs at 90 per cent then the result of five tasks may be only 50 per cent of the target! A series of simulations in practice can convey this experientially to a group of trainees to appreciate from their own narratives that 90 per cent is not good enough when others' lives are involved. The effort to improve to 95 per cent for the group now takes on additional meaning and significance. Each participant has a story showing how interdependency impacts others. They are fine-tuned to listening to others' stories and are a lot more receptive than ever before. The group knows it must strive for 98 per cent in simulation if it is to achieve 95 per cent in reality. Checklists take on new meaning.

Suddenly, the stories of each participant have become

invaluable learning materials to the others. None of them can be dismissed as a fairy tale or discounted as less relevant. The facts are far more meaningful when packaged with the right emotions. Personalized stories stay with you for timely recall.

⌘

The Right Thing at the Right Time

I was posted as a young engineer in the 1970s at Munger, Bihar, in the Packaging & Printing factory of ITC Ltd, a unit that was commissioned in 1925. An old cigarette factory, ITC's first in India from 1907, operated in a common factory complex with the printing factory. They shared power, water, effluents, warehousing and security. The printing factory was the smaller unit, with approximately one-fourth the number of workmen.

The factory was put up in Munger because the first tobacco plantations were nearby in Dalsinghsarai. This was long before Andhra and Karnataka started to grow, and gradually dominate, leaf-tobacco growing. Munger was known for its high crime rate, kidnapping and gun ownership. Gun making skills were passed on from father to son in a time-honoured tradition despite the government's efforts to consolidate the trade in a Government Gun Factory. The Ganga River was Munger's timeless attraction. Kashtaharni Ghat was famous for its virtue in washing away your worries and sins in the holy river if you volunteered to take a dip! The closest professional organization was the Railways in Jamalpur, five kilometres away, along with the Railway Institute which trained omnibus engineers. The School of Yoga came up later and put Munger on the international map.

The ITC Munger campus was a world of its own. We all lived in a park for the managers, with houses named after high points of history of the tobacco business—such as Raleigh, Virginia, Southampton, Egham, Embassy Court, Thames, Millbank and so on. The club was a major gathering point and the cricket field, tennis courts and swimming pool a call to fitness. There was no TV. Newspapers arrived a day late.

The trade union office-bearers and representatives were predominantly from the larger cigarette factory. They also tended to be senior in age and experience and more vocal in the long-term agreements that were signed periodically. At a point of time in the late '70s/early '80s the Union was grappling in the courts, with its own breakaway group clamouring for recognition. Union elections had not taken place for several years after 1977. The personnel manager, A.B. Mukherjee, innovated a method of signing mini-settlements bilaterally with the existing office bearers to keep the wheels moving.

The printing factory was under pressure to raise output but was hamstrung by not being able to import or bring in machinery easily and also being unable to recruit more employees midstream between Long Term Agreements. I sounded my boss. Could we run continuously with staggered meal breaks and hand over running machines at shift changeovers?

He was keen, but explained the difficulty likely to be raised by the personnel department about signing mini settlements without benefits for the entire worker population of the complex, especially where a change in work practice was involved. The personnel manager felt it would be difficult to sell the idea but agreed to test it out with the Union office-bearers. A meeting was held to share the idea and as anticipated, the proposal was rejected as being too radical. Subsequent meetings also met with the same response as the benefits were not applicable to the entire constituency.

I was casually sharing my disappointment with a few workmen in the printing factory when they expressed curiosity as to what it was all about. I expanded the idea and they seemed receptive. They asked casually what compensation they could expect, with a little testing smile on their faces! I explained that this would have to be negotiated with the Union and the personnel department. I shared the interaction with my boss and asked him if I could pursue this dialogue further. He set up a meeting with the personnel manager and I got the green signal to try—but was warned not to hope for much progress. An HR manager, resource, B.K. Sinha, from the personnel department, was assigned to help me. I was warned of the risks of excessive direct communication with workmen and the likely misgivings of the office-bearers.

The Human Side of Enterprise

We started talking to small groups, seeking to embed the idea in frank and simple exchanges. Some of the workmen were happy to be consulted, some protested outright that it was not practical and others said they'd consult the Union office-bearers. Some asked how much they would get, and a few refused to comment or share an opinion.

Over two months, the progress seemed poor with the subject oscillating over the same doubts back and forth endlessly across approximately 400 workmen of the printing factory. The experienced union office-bearers smiled wryly as if to say, 'We told you so', and the personnel manager shrugged his shoulders. Meanwhile, the pressure for higher outputs from the printing factory steadily built up as it was supplying to five of the cigarette factories across India.

A pesky workman, during discussions, threw a challenge at me. What would I do next if their hearts were willing and the compensation was attractive? I explained that 400 workmen could not be bundled into a conference room in the personnel department for negotiations.

This aspect too went through back and forth until it was agreed that the factory would not shut at any point of time, but 30–40 workmen across shifts would join the negotiations in the personnel department. The very first such meeting ended in pandemonium. There was a struggle with everybody trying to speak at the same time. Some shouted to make a point, some debated and negated whatever was said, some others were bemused as they had heard tall stories about what took place behind closed doors. Some protested that mundane details were being discussed and that a quick, hefty compensation across the board would resolve all problems.

It was necessary, however, to proceed step by step and cover the *modus operandi* of implementation to avoid surprises and shock later. The office-bearers were not in favour of so much participation by so many, setting a bad precedent in the complex. They shared their reservations with the personnel manager that the process was chaotic and would lead to unrealistic expectations. However, I felt strongly that clarity would improve after initial misgivings and fairy tale expectations of compensation. So, we persisted despite the ups and downs of such meetings.

I noticed, along with Sinha from personnel, that osmosis was slowly taking place. Talks continued in the negotiation room and information filtered back to employees as to what was going on with various versions doing their rounds. Many checked with me if what they'd heard was true. Some sought more details of how it would be for various departments and services within the factory. Some sought clarifications as to who would go out and when during staggered meal breaks. Toilet breaks were a point of concern too as some employees had the habit of disappearing for long periods of time. Some raised doubts about taking over running machines when work/machine allocation was in progress at the beginning of the shift to cope with unplanned absenteeism without leave.

With some setbacks, a lurch and a twist, the negotiations picked up momentum suddenly. Participation had reached a threshold and now people wanted to see a conclusion and get some monetary benefits instead of being paralysed by endless talks. Likely compensation figures became an integral part of the osmosis. Issues such as who would be most affected by the changes and what benefits should flow to support functions was discussed, alternatives were patiently sought from those who did not agree.

The office-bearers remained distant but watchful. The General Secretary told me that even if he signed the mini settlement, he could not take responsibility for its faithful implementation. He advised me that the milieu of Bihar needed to be understood and likewise the challenges of trade unionism. He had seen so many ups and downs over his lifetime with so many of my predecessors! My heart sank. I considered retreating gracefully before it was too late.

However, a groundswell of consensus was building up among the 400 workmen who felt involved in a matter concerning them and their future. They were participating in shaping their own destiny. They were eager to conclude the negotiation process now that they had reasonable clarity on how the changes would be implemented and what benefits would flow to them. They were not too bothered if the general secretary and vice-president signed the mini settlement as long as the key elements discussed with them were honoured.

At this stage, an employee of the printing factory, who had a chargesheet filed against him on an unrelated, disciplinary matter, wrote a complaint to the chief inspector of factories in Patna, that he was not being given his break or time to go the toilet, and that he was likely to face excruciating work conditions if a proposed agreement was signed, bartering away all meal breaks and toilet breaks. The deputy chief inspector of factories came on an inspection based on this complaint and walked the shop floor, seeking clarifications as to how machines would run during staggered meal breaks and toilet breaks and how running machines would be handed over to incoming crews at shift changeovers. He seemed satisfied that the roster was feasible and practical enough and that toilet breaks could be managed by the machine crews. Matters got delayed by another month. In a sense, his visit also became a stamp of approval from an impartial authority, thanks to an unexpected complaint that was intended to torpedo the negotiations.

The mini-settlement was implemented on the first day after the office-bearers and all concerned employees had signed. Outputs soared. Every successive month improved results further as employees settled into the rhythm of the changes. Against a 10 per cent expected improvement we were clocking above 30 per cent. The objective had been achieved at a fraction of the cost and time, compared to other alternatives. It was an eye-opener for me too. In the 1920s, at Western Electric's Hawthorne, Chicago plant, certain experimental results called the Hawthorne Effect were derived: that people will change their behaviour because the effects of their behaviour were being evaluated or studied.

The Hawthorne Effect was working in Munger. People felt consulted, valued and respected, and felt like they had real influence on the changes planned and negotiated, changes that affected their areas of work. The negotiated benefits were important, but what was more noteworthy was the increase in a sense of self-esteem and self-fulfillment due to being involved in the process of affecting change.

∞

 Management is about leadership—of people, of ideas, of markets. It is not merely about how far you go, and not about doing what you are told to do; it is about doing what you are paid to do. Managers need to remind themselves about this eternal truth.

Courage is not just another leadership quality like intelligence, compassion and determination. It is the iron ladder on which all the other virtues sit. Without this iron ladder, other virtues will not be effective.

The quality of this ladder of courage is determined and defined by you—it is what you live by.

Courage is not only for the CEO or the iconic top layer; it is about the everyday things that a manager does at his organization. The story of a senior manager, Praveen, is instructive.

At his retirement function, his colleagues had assembled for a company dinner as was the tradition. The evening programme was progressing predictably. When the speeches began, I thought to myself, 'This will be really predictable'.

Praveen first said the usual stuff—gratitude to his colleagues, apologies to those he had offended inadvertently and a promise to keep in touch. Suddenly, Praveen's speech turned very different.

> As you know, my role for several years has been to co-ordinate capital sanctions. Many of you have probably felt that I asked too many questions and retarded the speed of capital expenditure. I have made known my view that, in recent years, we as managers have become lax about capital expenditure. We install equipment and then fail to use it the way we had planned to. Cash is the most important resource in any company, and we all know that our company gobbles cash up for capital expenditure. My career may have suffered because I was perceived as being responsible for slowing down expenditure. But I feel satisfied that due to my efforts, along with all of you, the company saved XYZ crores of valuable cash in the last five years. Who knows, if I had allowed the money to be spent more easily we would have saved XYZ crores less, and maybe I would have gotten another promotion! Personally, I am proud of this contribution. I am satisfied that I acted in a particular way because I was paid to do so.

And then he sat down—a few seconds of dead silence later, there was a huge round of applause.

If we analyse his speech in the format of academic thinkers, Merom Klein and Rod Napier (*The Courage to Act*), Praveen demonstrated the power of the CPWRR formula—candour, purpose, will, rigour, risk—in discharging his everyday duties.

Candour means the quality of speaking out in a constructive and contributing way. Speaking out in a criticizing and carping way is unproductive.

Purpose is about pursuing ambitious goals. Praveen realized that his industry was a cash burner, that even at his level within the company, he could contribute to the judicious usage of cash. He could have taken the easy option of leaving it to his bosses.

Will is the ability to inspire optimism. Praveen brought alternatives to the table. He did not merely ask 'clever' questions. He added energy to the role he was playing.

Rigour means the discipline to put a process in place. Praveen insisted that the justification for expenditure should follow a predetermined format. In the process, he was perceived as bureaucratic.

Risk is the willingness to trust others to do their bit, while accepting the consequences of your own actions.

It is not enough to have three or four of the CPWRR formula. All five need to work together, a bit like the cylinders of a motorcar.

The story shows that courage is an everyday thing that common managers can practise.

∽

Mention the word 'courage' and it sparks images of people persevering with valour under adverse conditions, of Param Vir Chakras and Param Vishisht Seva Medals and decorations of gallantry. While society needs to applaud examples of extraordinary bravery in battle or in situations of calamity or national emergency such as a terrorist attack, there are innumerable examples even in management where courage is required. However, there could be risks to reputation or the risk of possible failure, however small. If there is overwhelming certainty about facts, the decision becomes simpler. Invariably, management is faced with partial facts and figures under conditions of uncertainty, and under time pressure.

Courage is required at the individual level when confronted with less than 100 per cent facts, with time running out. Courage is required to take decisions to move forward and to sometimes pause and reflect and change direction if things do not go as planned. Courage is required to speak up and explain a point of view that can lead to better decisions for the group. Courage is required to accept a mistake or error in judgement and accept responsibility fairly to set an example for better decision making.

Management inherently involves large teams that consist of several small teams. The vectors become more complex as we cut across functions and departments and hierarchies and sometimes across businesses within a conglomerate. Yet the requirements of courage feature at every level and in every context. Every action takes place in a competitive market scenario where shareholder and stakeholder satisfaction compete for timely attention.

How does leadership get exercised in organizations and what role does it play in enhancing performance? How does an organization pick good leaders and groom them for higher responsibilities? How does all this fit in with succession planning right up to the level of the Board of Directors and the role of the Nominations & Remunerations Committees of the Board?

The Board of Directors has undergone major changes in governance, especially from the days of the Cadbury Report of 1992. The Bhopal gas leak of 1984, the Exxon Valdez oil spill of 1989, Enron going belly-up in 2001 and the Lehman Bros shock of 2008 are milestones in corporate history that have compelled companies and stakeholders across the world to pay better attention to issues of governance.

The Ministry of Corporate Affairs (MCA) and SEBI have

kept pace with updating of India Inc's governance practices. A Whistleblower Policy and a Sexual Harassment Policy are mandatory. A two per cent expenditure on CSR has also become mandatory.

The number of independent directors has steadily increased on the Boards of Directors compared to the twentieth century, when more executive directors were the norm. The number of independent directors should be one-third to half the total number of Directors on the Board, depending upon whether the chairman is non-executive or executive. At least two women directors are required on the Board.

The idea is to ensure that Boards of Directors do not become insular clubs of insiders lacking objectivity about decisions to which executive directors are party. The excessive focus on shareholder wealth is attributed as a reason for ignoring environmental concerns. The wide use of derivatives and off-balance sheet masking and poor disclosure of related party transactions and lack of transparency in reporting have been other criticisms. These triggered the strengthening of the Audit Committee and Nominations & Remunerations Committee of Boards and led to better regulatory compliances.

Courage remains a key component despite changes of structure and governance codes. It is assumed that worry over company hierarchy will not hinder non-executive directors and independent directors from expressing dissent at Board meetings on poor decisions or lapses in governance beyond statutory compliance. Anomalies do exist with respect to their appointment by the chairman especially if it is the executive chairman. Boards routinely tend to endorse the suggestions of the chairman or promoter non-executive chairman. Nominee directors representing institutional shareholders are often offered the carrot of continuity (post their retirement from their parent institutions) as independent directors if they are cooperative. The Nominations & Remunerations Committee is hampered by its lack of knowledge and exposure to managers a few levels down in the hierarchy and tends to endorse the chairman's suggestion. When it comes to planning the succession of the chairman, the entire Board is tongue-tied and wary of discussing the subject openly in the chairman's presence, as it is sensitive and may upset them.

The independent directors can meet at least once a year on their own without the presence of executive directors and the chairman, but this turns out to be routine, bypassing controversies. The appraisals of the chairman and the directors are supposed to happen, but these become another formality to be ticked off the list of compliances. The regulators, both the MCA and the SEBI, do not regulate pre-emptively to improve the quality of governance but react only when the crisis is full blown and already controversial in the media or undergoing a CBI enquiry.

To use a medical analogy, everybody wakes up only when the patient is wheeled into the operation theatre from an ambulance with lights flashing and sirens blaring or immediately after a crisis event at the ICU stage. By then, it is already too late to prevent disaster or heart attack. The same occurs here where people wake up after the damage has occurred, causing drastic consequences for banks, employees and shareholders.

Success in management requires courage to address such controversial issues at the right time, and across the organizational hierarchy. It is quite clear that there are many exhortations down the line to management, but Boards have lacked the courage to address such issues at the Board of Directors level and have only responded reluctantly to statutory changes.

For Effective Communication

It is so important to understand the intent behind the words during appraisals. Yet, appraisees listen to what they want to listen to, often to their great disadvantage. A common complaint heard in company corridors pertains to the company's appraisal system and the quality of feedback to the manager from his superior. Whatever is done, it never seems to be good enough. Improving on this aspect is a constant effort everywhere, all the time.

The theoretical characteristics of the 'ideal' appraisal system are known. The feedback message must contain comments with examples and suggestions for improvement. The message must be delivered in a positive environment, in a context of trust. Implementing this correctly is very complicated.

35-year-old Sharma used to work in my department. He was a competent engineer and could solve technical problems reliably. He had two characteristics: first, that he was forever critical of other colleagues and departments; second, that he was supremely confident that he could run a business. I often wished he would be more realistic. I often tried to delicately insinuate these suggestions, bearing in mind that he was a very sensitive individual.

In the natural course of our careers, he and I moved into other parts of the company. We began to work together again after several years. By this time, there was a senior manager between his position and mine. Sharma would drop in occasionally for a chat. Most of the time he would enquire about the family and talk of our earlier work experiences, and I would spend some social time with him.

On one such occasion, Sharma complained that his immediate boss had been ambiguous during his performance feedback. As a result, he felt that he was not being considered for advancement to a general management position. He felt aggrieved. I told him that his boss was better equipped to give him more direct feedback.

When I broached the subject with Sridhar, Sharma's boss, he insisted that he had given his feedback, which was admittedly delicate, as he did not wish to damage Sharma's self-esteem by being too direct. However, he agreed to try once again. Sridhar had felt that Sharma's execution capability was limited by his inability to get along with peers and other departments. As a result, his boss felt that Sharma had become part of the problem, not a part of the solution.

After three weeks, Sharma arrived in my office in a rather depressed condition. He said Sridhar had been 'brutal in his feedback' and surely there was no need to make a big deal out of one's supposed shortcomings! I was amazed. I could not help pointing out that it was he who had sought more direct feedback.

'Of course, that is true. But that does not mean that you make me feel incapable and isolated,' he insisted. I found it difficult to agree with him, particularly because Sridhar was regarded in the company as one of the most humane and caring managers. I suggested that perhaps he was not ready for direct feedback, though he had stated that it was what he had wanted.

'But what is your view? You have known me for long,' he persisted. I said that I had participated in the appraisal and concurred with what had been said. Sharma was crestfallen. 'Well, I have to think about my future,' he said remorsefully as he left my room. Sharma left the company to do jobs in a couple of outside companies. Since he was in touch with me for advice and counselling, I could observe that he was not achieving as much happiness as he expected, hence not much success.

All managers say that they want 'frank and open feedback'. In reality, most are unprepared for it. The best feedback is often obtained not from what is stated explicitly, but from what is not stated.

If a manager can learn to look at the big picture that the feedback is offering, then he allows himself to accept feedback without damaging his ego and self-esteem. It is a skill to be cultivated.

∞

 The human resource function has come a long way from the days of evaluating strengths and weaknesses in appraisals. In an interesting argument, the use of the word weakness, in appraisals, was termed demotivating. It seemed to convey that there were permanent and indelible marks not amenable to change. The language used in appraisals while giving feedback was often perceived as being objectionable by the appraisee,

while his boss felt he was being helpfully accurate in his feedback:

- You are too soft and undemanding about results
- Your abrasive style rubs your subordinates and peers the wrong way
- You focus on short term results but ignore the development of subordinates
- You behave as if replying to mail or an email is good enough
- You do not plan for contingencies adequately
- You don't do enough to harness other people's feedback and ideas
- Your time management is poor

Skills in giving and receiving feedback become important. Behavioural science workshops were often held to improve skills in this area. The earlier T-Labs were too cathartic and gave way to Interpersonal Effectiveness Workshops where some time was unstructured. The process was facilitated by a trained behavioural science professional. The intent was to buttress soft skills, in addition to strengthening knowledge and practical skills which could be measured more easily.

The results at ITC Ltd, where I worked, were mixed despite commendable efforts to raise the sensitivity and skills of the entire managerial population. The word weakness, was changed in appraisal forms to 'area for improvement' as a first step in encouraging the appraisee to do something about it rather than feel that he was facing judgment that he could not change. This worked for a while and then ran up against the premonition that it was only a stepping stone to a final rating, which determined monetary compensation and/or led to a promotion.

Appraisals were made more frequent to reduce the chances of surprises at the end of the year and as a way to give regular feedback in accordance with ongoing events.

The Normal Distribution

Fitting performance ratings into a bell-shaped curve or normal distribution became another complex exercise. There was no doubt that outstanding performers had to be rewarded and those consistently not measuring up to expectations had to be separated from the system. The major challenges of motivation lay in the middle zone, where the majority of the population figured. The tentatively committed performers had to move forward for the mean performance level to shift towards the right.

Doing away entirely with the normal distribution could be fraught with other consequences. Bosses managed the system by marking upwards during their tenures. His successor would have to deal with *prima donnas* who felt that they should have been promoted already. The slot available on the appraisal form for potential was the most complex.

Who can claim to see so far ahead or decide to choke off further efforts at improving a reluctant horse?

It was clear that a good salesman may not be as good as a supervisor or a manager. A good general manager in one division may seem out of sorts when asked to handle several businesses. A competent executive director may grapple with new demands of corporate governance that have undergone a sea of change since his time as a senior manager. At the Board of Directors level, the sensitivity of completing appraisals for all directors, including the chairman and non-executive directors, seems even more daunting despite mandates in the

Companies' Act and SEBI regulations.

The appraisee grapples somewhat uncomfortably with feedback—aspects about oneself not known to the self are highlighted by a superior while the appraisee copes with their performance rating. The techniques helped people understand their relationship with others and allowed them to gain insight into how their behaviour affected their relationship with other people. That awareness did not necessarily help them change their own behaviours but certainly made them more aware of how they may affect others.

Competency mapping became a logical development and good work has been achieved in this area. The interplay of knowledge-skills-behaviours sets the tone right with respect to appreciating that behaviours affect results too. There may still be issues with respect to accepting that one's behaviours can be interpreted differently by others.

Moving up the hierarchy, as people hold leadership positions, their behaviours have a far-reaching impact on people. The behavioural competencies required at higher levels differ and may present difficult to learn afresh at a later stage in life. An executive chairman and CEO may find that his stellar performance as an executive director has led to his elevation but what is required of him in this new role demands a different set of competencies in unexpected areas. It can even leave him feeling vulnerable and quite lonely at the top. A strong opinion expressed by him at a meeting sends a torrent of messages down the system with unintentional consequences. At other times, his silence paradoxically sends a message through the system as well.

A lighter, balanced touch at the helm may be required to get the best out of people by not jumping in to answer all the questions, however competent and knowledgeable they may have been in the past. To this, one must add competencies required to get the best out of the Board of Directors, a majority of whom are non-executive directors with little familiarity with the company. It requires skills and finesse to get independent directors to be independent and speak up and participate in discussions objectively. Managing shareholders and investors can take up disproportionate time and energy and test one's patience, sometimes in nettlesome ways. Curtailing dissent is unproductive and damaging in the long run.

Appraising Potential

How can the Board of Directors equip itself to assess the depth of management talent two or three levels down the hierarchy, knowing what competencies may be required a few years later? Succession planning requires better discussion and judgement from the Nominations Committee rather than a cursory approval of what is placed on the table by the executive management. Are the non-executive directors experienced in top-management succession? The answer is likely to be in the negative. Will they muster the courage to raise the issue in the presence of the current chairman and debate alternatives seriously in a separate meeting of the independent directors? Again, the answer is likely to be in the negative. If they owe their appointment to the chairman, it follows a sense of feeling obligated.

The answers are not simple or straightforward. We can appreciate so far that corporate life still must go on and decisions must be taken, and the best sought to be done despite the inherent pitfalls of human beings exercising some power and judgement under time pressure. The direction is more important than the distance travelled as the goalposts may keep shifting over a lifetime, based on market realities.

Take an example from military history. Dwight D. Eisenhower was not a general with the best track record in terms of fighting experience. Yet Eisenhower was rightly chosen as the Supreme Allied Commander of the Allied Forces during WW II. That he had the skills to cut across multinational military groups was a positive; that he had the behavioural skills to manage temperamental but competent generals and Field Marshals was his strength. His ability to reach out in a simple way and talk to his troops before D-Day is warmly recalled by historians. That he could manage an ambitious Montgomery without reacting to his tantrums is a tribute to his skills. That he continued to keep learning and adapting on the run and served two consecutive terms as the president of the US in a completely different job from anything that he had been used to before, is his outstanding characteristic.

It may be said, in retrospect, that if the direction is right, then success and growth will naturally follow.

∽

Disagree, Don't Be Disagreeable

 In the course of your work, you may or may not always agree with your boss. If you fail to express your disagreement, you can be deemed to have failed the test of professionalism. If you express your view, then the boss may not like it. How do you navigate this treacherous pathway? The question is not whether you were right or wrong. In the end, the onus invariably is on the less powerful to figure this out, not on the person who is the boss. The narrative below illustrates this point.

I had worked my way up through ITC's hierarchy across several divisions and businesses and was a senior member of the Corporate Management Committee (CMC). I had five CEOs out of 13 business CEOs reporting to me by 2001. Just as things were looking up for me and my career, a sudden strike and violence at a Chennai factory weighed me down from becoming an executive director.

Again, in the year 2009–10 my five businesses had done extremely well and performed above budget. An independent director rang me in January 2010 to privately congratulate me on my rise to the Board of Directors of ITC Ltd as recommended by the Nominations Committee of the Board a few days before that. It felt good to be recognized, albeit late. I thanked him and said I'd keep it confidential until it was formally communicated to me.

And then suddenly, things went awry.

On 6 February 2010, at a budget meeting in Kolkata of the safety matches business, the chairman asked me for an opinion on the closure of two safety match factories, each of which had more than 250 workmen. I replied that this had been discussed by the senior team whilst preparing the business budget and that we felt it was too drastic if the purpose was to trim costs and run more efficiently.

The chairman reacted violently and exclaimed that I could not continue as the non-executive chairman of Wimco Ltd, the safety matches subsidiary of ITC. He felt that I should step down immediately, only for having disagreed so openly. I explained that closure decisions should not be hastily taken and, in any case, merited the primary attention of the Wimco Board of Directors who had not yet been consulted. He thumped the table and indicated that the board of Wimco was irrelevant, and all decisions emanated from him. I disagreed on a point of form and process.

To cut a long story short, events moved in quick succession thereafter and I was prematurely retired in an arbitrary manner. It is not relevant at this stage to exhume the past or plunge into an analysis of what went right and what went wrong. The derived learning, however, must be to disagree without being disagreeable. The detail of how best one could put forward one's disagreement is always contextual to the meeting and the personalities. Could it have been arrogance on my part?

I don't believe that I was strutting around boastfully talking arrogantly about my successes. I was genuinely happy for the teams who had worked hard to post achievements above targets, despite challenging conditions; they deserved congratulations. There are moments of success and setbacks throughout one's life and career. There are very few who have it smooth and successful all the way and all the time.

We should view every milestone with eagerness, but also a sense of trepidation. It is imperative that we put our best foot forward and do our best in every competitive endeavour. Yet it is inevitable that despite our best effort, things may not go right sometimes. Bouncing back with equanimity seems like a contradiction, yet that is what we need to learn and sharpen as a skill.

What about the converse? Things are going well and the applause from people around you seems warm and appealing. The next phase goes even better and the success trajectory seems unbeatable. Advisers tell you not to change a winning strategy and skeptics say it is a matter of time before luck runs out and things turn bad. The encomiums you receive crown you with success and you bask in the public limelight.

At a sub-conscious level, the issue may be with one's reactions to news of success. You can get carried away and do more of the same or take an even bigger risk. Or you can conclude too soon that good luck does not last forever and that you should pull out safely before the winning streak fizzles out. Or you can get carried away with the applause and lose your sense of balance.

Moral science stories advise us to be humble in victory and gracious in defeat and to praise one's opponents and never to denigrate them or underestimate their abilities. A few maxims do the rounds repeatedly:

- ◆ You win some, you lose some
- ◆ Don't exult in victory, don't grieve in defeat
- ◆ Pride comes before a fall

- ◆ Play the game to the best of your ability, irrespective of success or defeat

All these have timeless validity and touch upon facets of the subject in slightly different ways. The key takeaway is to concentrate on the task at hand, irrespective of perceptions about whether you are staring at success or failure.

It is like people often say, 'Live in the present, not in the past or the future!'

∽

 I had a career dilemma in 1991, when I was posted as the head of Unilever's newly formed company in Arabia. The experience itself is not unique and almost every reader would have experienced something similar.

One business challenge was to enter the Arabian detergent market against a very dominant and well-entrenched competitor, P&G Arabia. Rather unusually, Unilever had virtually no washing detergent business in the Arabian Peninsula at the time, though very successful brands had been established over several decades in personal wash, skincare and tea categories.

Ever since detergent powders began to be produced commercially, they have been made through a process called spray drying. The structure of the finished powder is like a balloon—a light globule puffed up with air. The cleaning and other chemical agents are in that globule. The cardboard boxes in which such products were packed were large due to the fluffy nature of the powder inside.

During the late '80s, a revolution in detergent manufacturing occurred in Japan: the long-standing, big boxes were replaced by compact packages. The Japanese detergent market got dramatically restructured.

In this new format of the product, much of the air in the 'globule' was removed and the resultant powder was more compact and denser. Apart from occupying less space on the retail shelf, compacts had other advantages: they needed less capital costs for production, less paperboard for packaging, less warehouse space in the distribution system and more tonnage could be loaded on transport trucks.

Such packs had recently been introduced in Europe and as of 1990, they seemed to be gaining some ground at the expense of standard, big-boxed detergents. How much of the sales of the standard detergents in Europe would be replaced by the compact one, was an open question. Would Arabia also go the Japan way?

Being a late entrant in the Arabian detergent market, against a formidably entrenched competitor, Unilever had to be audacious. For at least three years before I joined the company which was to execute the project, the planners had worked on launching a compact. Such a product would provide a point of differentiation with the traditional products already in the market apart from offering distinct consumer benefits. Such differentiation was essential if any dent was to be made against a powerful and well-entrenched P&G. All of this was very logical, and I could not fault the thinking. In fact, there was a lot of market research to support the validity of such an approach.

My Dilemma

I was a first-time company CEO, that too of Unilever, in a foreign country. I felt a huge pressure on myself to be successful, and that meant getting the launch right. As I went through the persuasive market research and the well-argued business case, my gut instinct began to tell me the opposite of the analysis: that the product was unlikely to succeed and that the route contemplated was risky. I could not explain why, but I felt it in my bones. Arabia was not at all like Japan or even Europe.

As part of my induction into the company and the new country, I had walked around the bazaars in Jeddah, Riyadh and other cities to observe how consumers behaved. I was seeing things from a new and different perspective. I had observed that Arabian shops, roads, homes and other places had a lot of space—quite unlike Japan. As I walked around the markets, I felt that consumers liked everything big—cars, toys, clothing, housing, furniture and so on. The saving on packaging or transportation costs for a detergent seemed irrelevant in a cheap-energy economy. Yet, the research was not saying these things clearly.

I had long discussions with my senior colleague, who too was torn between the analysis available and his intuition. The question we both faced was: what do we do with our intuition? I was assailed by self-doubt. Could all the bright managers who had formulated the plan have missed something so elementary? Or was it I who was failing by believing what I wanted to believe?

We all tend to interpret data through the prism of the dominantly prevalent view about how the future will turn out. There was a battle between my logical self and my intuitive self. To my intuitive mind, there appeared to be too many risks in entering with a compact product. Since there was no spare capacity for producing the new-fangled product, the fledgling company would have to invest in building the required production capacity in order to launch. If the product failed, we would have compounded our problem by having an idle factory! On the other hand, there was plenty of spare capacity around to source the standard detergent from third parties, and to launch it in the market with far lower risk.

I had become a director at Hindustan Lever prior to taking up this assignment. It was tempting to think of myself as an 'accomplished and tested' manager. It was equally clear to me that, in rational terms, just a wee bit of whatever I had learnt in India would be helpful for the Arabian assault. I was anxious about my new job, to be honest, if not a bit scared.

The desire to succeed in the assignment was strong because I was a first-time company CEO. I took copious notes of all sorts of observations and pored over them for long hours. I was assailed by doubts over whether doing such things was a waste of time. This desire fanned my sense of intuition. I was inherently a believer in intuition, and such faith itself perhaps caused me to search for things beyond the obvious. For some reason, I continued to dawdle. I was now in unknown territory, and I had no choice except taking a few planned risks.

There was some risk in asking for a meeting with the two main board directors, who had supervised the preparatory work thus far, to share a counter-intuition and to ask for a change in plan! Likewise, it was a bit of a career risk to argue in support of the business case and the consequent significant investment before the apex special committee of Unilever just four months into the new job. There was no space for diffidence and, in hindsight, the situation demanded that I be self-aware.

I felt the strong urge to share our assessment with the regional director and the global detergents director. However, I was hesitant to do so. What would they think of us, arguing against analytical data with just a gut feeling?

Finally, I found the courage to set up a joint meeting with them at Unilever House in London. They seemed intrigued that I had sought a meeting and wondered what I wanted to convey. Would they listen to me patiently? Would they be amused that I was sharing a serious business thought, based on intuition?

They heard me out carefully. They sort of cleared their throat, perhaps figuring out how to respond. If they accepted what my intuition was saying, the painstakingly constructed Unilever plan spread over three years would have to be set aside, and a sort of fresh start made. They were prepared to do so. But was I right? If they rejected my view outright, they would be ignoring the instinct of the local manager.

After a few questions and responses, the regional director said, 'Let us go ahead with belt and braces. We can modify our plan. Let us outsource from a third party and launch a standard detergent first (not originally envisaged) and follow it up within 18 months with an own-factory-produced compact (as originally planned).'

Truth be told, it was a compromise, accurately captured in the expression, 'belt and braces'. To me, at that time, it seemed like a fair compromise. That was what we did.

My memory of the event is that I had disagreed without being disagreeable.

∞

Experiencing an Experience

 I think it was Aldous Huxley, who said something like, 'Experience is what you do with whatever happens to you'. Here, I share a couple of my own experiences.

When I was 16, my family moved from Kolkata to another city. Since I had to stay in college to continue my education, my father assigned me the concurrent task of settling a court case regarding the house, auctioning the furniture and depositing the sale proceeds in the local bank.

This was not what my peers were doing, so I did it a bit reluctantly. I had to build a relationship with diverse characters like the lawyer, the auctioneer, the court officials. Above all, it imposed on me the task of gaining a rudimentary understanding of the issues involved and figuring out the best solution. Telephones between Kolkata and other cities did not work too well in the early '60s, so the frequency of parental consultation was minimal.

At first, I felt sorry for myself. My friends were walking around on Park Street, and here I was, running around boring places like courts, lawyer offices and auction houses. But in retrospect I realize, I learnt a lot from that experience.

Through the activities that I had to undertake, I learnt what responsibility is: taking charge and understanding complex matters sufficiently enough to act. Such opportunities are commonplace in everybody's life and there is much to be learnt by grasping those diligently rather than dealing with them casually or as a burden to be discharged in the least engaged way.

Many years later, I was the regional sales manager of Hindustan Lever for north India. I was quite kicked about my career progress and was probably in need of a lesson in humility—of course, I did not think so at that time.

The company had launched a detergent powder and I was working with a local salesman, Narinder Sood, on the retail beat in Jalandhar. All of 27, I said to the 55-year-old experienced salesman that his merchandizing and product displays could be better. He was a union leader, he had a reputation of being a bit impudent. He politely requested me to demonstrate the higher quality of work I was seeking.

I had three choices. I could take umbrage and pull him up. I could let the matter pass, almost as though it had just not happened. I could take him up on his 'challenge.'

I felt I had to seize the gauntlet he had thrown and spent the next two hours in the bazaar doing sales calls, merchandizing and product displays. My work was certainly not superior, but that was not the point of the experience. He probably wanted to test whether I would dirty my hands. Later he demonstrated appreciation of my effort and became a warm colleague.

I learnt from this experience that for any leader, the wellspring of humility lie in the field with the men one is privileged to lead. If you cannot do what you ask your men to do, if you cannot experience their pain and pangs of the workplace, you cannot develop empathy for them. You cannot lead them successfully.

Any potential leader must develop empathy for their subordinates.

ॐ

Song behind the Words

For several years I have conducted an informal exercise whenever I meet managers in classrooms within the Tata group and elsewhere. I would write down two statements for each person to answer, either in the positive or in the negative. First, 'I am more competent at work than those who I consider my peers'. Second, 'I have better human relations compared to those who I consider my peers'.

Statistical logic would suggest that the aggregate of all the answers received over a period should be around 50 per cent, if the competent managers who attend, compare themselves to competent peers. I got a number close to 80 per cent, which means that most people thought they were better than others. This is the 'I am better than others' trap which every person is prone to fall into.

According to common sense, managers and, indeed all human beings, tend to hold overly favourable views of their abilities in many social and intellectual fields. For the doubters, there is evidence to back this view. This apparently simple research finding, points to two dangers that confront every manager. The first is the obvious danger that you are prone to exaggerate your strengths and play down your weaknesses when you compare yourself to others. The second is the danger that by not being aware of this tendency, you are likely to miss whatever feedback and signals come to you.

It is a common trap for us to overestimate our strengths and to underestimate our weaknesses. This is the root cause of indignation on being passed over for a promotion and it also triggers the resentful perception of getting less favor and attention from the boss when compared to a colleague. It is a universal trap. Associated with this basic trap are several other traps: arrogance, insensitivity, envy and many more.

It is difficult for a manager to shake off her traps or dark spots. At best, she can become aware of their existence and learn to manage them.

Very little is told to you by your boss or colleagues about the negative manifestations of your traps. Why should your peer do so when it is none of his business? And why should your senior do so and be regarded as a nagging senior? Why should your subordinate risk his career by doing so? Some traps do only minor damage, while some others do heavy damage. The positives and negatives progressively accumulate, and when taken together define who you are perceived to be.

To be aware of your traps, you must learn to listen and sense the effect you are having on others. People are constantly giving you feedback without intending to do so. Some are explicit, while most are implicit.

An up-and-coming executive learns to listen to the song behind the words.

Explicit Feedback

You can become aware of your dark spots by someone holding a mirror to your behaviour and by looking deeply into the mirror. I call the feedback received in this explicit manner, the Clementine mirror, named after the charming letter written by Clementine Churchill to her husband, Sir Winston.

Clementine Churchill was fiercely loyal to her husband, but she rebuked his excesses and tried to repair the fractured chain of his relationships. The country, as much as he, owed a debt to such a wife because she prevented Sir Winston from succumbing to the corruption of wielding absolute authority over the nation.

In June 1940, she wrote him a letter, held on to it for four days, tore up the letter, finally reconstructed the torn letter and then sent it. It lies in the archives in that condition and reading the letter tells us why she must have hesitated: remember there was a war going on and Sir Winston was the prime minister. The letter read as follows:

My darling, I hope you will forgive me if I tell you something that I feel you ought to know. One of the men in your entourage, a devoted friend, has been to me and told me that there is a danger of you being disliked by your colleagues and subordinates because of your rough, sarcastic and overbearing manner [...] If an idea is suggested, say at a conference, you are supposed to be so contemptuous that presently no idea, good or bad, will be forthcoming. I was astonished and upset because in all these years, I have been accustomed to all those who have worked with and under you, loving you—I said this and I was told 'No doubt it is the strain'.

My darling Winston, I must confess that I have noticed deterioration in your manner; you are not as kind as you used to be... It is for you to give orders, but with urbanity, kindness, and if possible, with Olympic calm... I cannot bear that those who serve the country and yourself should not love you as well as admire and respect you... Besides you won't get the best results by irascibility and rudeness...

'Please forgive your loving, devoted and watchful Clemmie.[4]

Wives are known to render a unique service to their husbands by telling them what no one else dares to. The explicit feedback that a leader can get from the spouse can be harsh, but very valuable.

There are also several techniques of 360-degree feedback available to modern managers. These techniques also offer a way to get feedback from colleagues. These too can be quite threatening to the manager.

Like coronavirus in a nearby person's breath spray can infect you, power can damage every leader. Most leaders learn to mitigate the effects, but those who don't, appear in the public glare. I use 'CEO' as a surrogate for senior business leaders in general. Power affects all.

A confession first: I have experienced the heady effects of power during my career and survived. Now, I can reflect dispassionately about power over employees, associates, boards and media. The increasing exits of 'magnetic' chieftains makes news: leaders at Kingfisher, Religare, ICICI, YES and IL&FS in India, Audi in Germany, WPP in UK, Danske Bank in Denmark, GE and TESLA in America.

What is going on? Changing expectations? Alert media? More forthrightness? Yes, all of that. The underlying cultural and psychological factors are relevant, so remedies also emanate there. The subject is highly topical now.

---

[4]https://winstonchurchill.org/publications/churchill-bulletin/bulletin-144-jun-2020/uxorial-advice/.

Power is like wealth. The more you chase it, the more destructive its capacity. Power corrupts, and absolute power corrupts absolutely.

Power reduces emotional capacity and damages the leader's brain. Power is akin to a strong magnetic field, disturbing the alignment of iron filings. This emotional incapacity manifests visibly—arrogance, pomposity, delusions of heroism, mad pursuit of visibility, not listening, treating people rudely and so on, leading to perceptions like 'This is not the same person we knew.' When the source of power is switched off, the leader may become nice again!

As a leader acquires power, physical and hormonal changes occur in the brain. My forthcoming book lists several studies, among them, is the work of Professor Landau from Chicago, Professor Pamela Smith from Netherlands and Professor Sukhvinder Singh Obhi at McMaster, Canada. Professor Obhi placed the heads of leaders under a trans-cranial magnetic stimulation (TCMS) machine to study what happens. Section 164 of the Companies Act requires that a CEO should not be of unsound mind. Future regulators may mandate that CEOs should be TCMS-tested every year and the results disclosed in the directors' report!

Their legal duties apart, some or all independent directors can serve as a walking voice for the powerful CEO. Experienced peer directors can do this because they are not mere watchdogs. They advise, coach and cajole CEOs. If they work, fine, or else, a director must warn, and, if necessary, quit because loyalty is to the institution, not to the leader.

The solution principally lies with the leader, who must take special care to listen and contemplate upon the walking inner voice, as King Vikramaditya did in mythology. Think about how Krishna spoke to Arjuna in the Mahabharata about duty and action, how Vibhishana confronted Ravana about the morality of executing Hanuman, and what Bagger Vance—distortion of Bhagawan—did for R (anulph) Junah—distortion of Arjuna— in the acclaimed film, *The Legend of Bagger Vance*, featuring Will Smith and Matt Damon respectively.

The walking voice counsels the roaming ego to listen, reflect and to stay grounded.

J.R.D. Tata reminded us that transformers lead with affection, 'I am the one who will make full allowance for a man's character and idiosyncrasies...at times, it involves suppressing yourself. It is painful but necessary...'

All said and done, there is great value in developing the skill to hear the song behind the words.

∞

Post-Match Cleanup

It is common in world sports for players to wash up after their match and leave the dressing room in varying levels of a mess, especially so, if they have lost the match. This occurs more in team matches like football and rugby, as compared to individual games.

In the 2018 football World Cup, the national football team of Japan lost a heartbreaking match to Belgium. They demonstrated decency and grace by not just cleaning up the locker room, but by leaving a thank you note for their Russian hosts. The team players then came out to face their supporters and humbly bowed to their fans. Naturally, all of this endeared the team to their hosts and the audience as a great lesson in grace even in the face of a disappointing defeat.

In the 2019 rugby World Cup, the act was repeated by the New Zealand, England and Wales teams. Quite uncharacteristically, these teams cleaned the dressing rooms and bowed to their supporters after their matches.

Surely, there is a lesson for managers, who do a job for a certain number of years and then move on to another job in the same company. What could the equivalent lesson be for management leaders?

Alibaba founder Jack Ma said recently that education should develop 'wise' people instead of 'bright and intelligent' people—the latter can get replaced by artificial intelligence and machines. Wisdom comes from experience and is learnt by the heart; wisdom is imprinted in the right brain unlike intelligence, which is a left brain imprint. Wise leaders give a thought to what they leave behind for their successor and colleagues.

Consider how business leaders tend to get judged versus how they ought to be judged. Of course, a leader should be evaluated for his or her impact on the department's performance. But these metrics are commonly calculated for the leader's precise tenure, and have an inbuilt flaw. For a period after taking charge, a leader's performance is influenced by the organizational momentum that the leader inherited. Likewise, after departure, the leader's successor inherits an organizational momentum. This momentum may be positive or negative. Hence, reading performance numbers for the leader's precise tenure gives an imprecise picture of the impact.

The impact of a leader on people and relationships is extremely important. This is difficult to measure and is admittedly subjective. Academics call the 'ways of knowing' as epistemology, and company bosses need epistemological information of a leader's people impact. Bosses should not fall into the trap described by Israeli economist and psychologist Daniel Kahneman as WYSIATI—What You See Is All There Is!

Has the leader's impact on people been effective and motivating or has it been fractious and turbulent? Recall superlative institutional leaders. How affectionately people regard J.R.D. Tata well after he departed from Air India or Tata! How warmly people regard Vikram Sarabhai at the Atomic

Energy Commission, Ravi Mathai at IIM-A or R.K. Talwar at State Bank of India! Keshub Mahindra of the Mahindra Group commands respect and love. In contrast, think of Vijay Mallya or Ranbaxy's Singh brothers.

Some years ago, in a discussion with a naval officer, I asked how one judges the quality of a ship, apart from the technical specifications. His reply was that an observer should note the 'wake' of the boat. I learned that wake is a boating term that is used to note the trail of disturbed water that a moving boat leaves. Some years later, I came across the writing of Coach Dr Henry Cloud, who compared a leader's impact on people to the wake of a boat. A leadership wake is like a boat that ploughs through the water. Some leave a smooth and symmetric pattern while others drench people and capsize other boats in seeming disregard of their impact. An effective leader should leave a wake which people recall with professional respect, while enhancing human dignity and emotion.

HUL chairmen, who change every decade, mostly left a positive wake; many got promoted into the parent board. Likewise has been the case with leadership transitions in Tata Consultancy Services, Titan Industries, Asian Paints and Pidilite Industries.

Long-tenure leaders are susceptible to behaving like God; they are so treated by those around. Intensive and in-the-face media reportage often works against quiet and efficient succession. Without a doubt, it is negative for sycophants and the media to gush that a leader is difficult to replace. My former boss used to say, walk around a graveyard and you will find many who thought they were irreplaceable! In recent years, certain high-profile leaders were lauded and feted as unmatched, but the wake that they left behind is now visible to all.

This happens globally as well. The legendary Jack Welch was a huge evangelist for performance and meritocracy. Yet, his tenure is a subject of contemporary commentary, long after his tenure. It is unfair to comment after two decades, but who can stop commentators! The iconic Walt Disney Company was led by Chairman Michael Eisner from 1984 to 2005. When Eisner retired in 2005, his successor, Bob Iger, successfully steered Disney into a hugely valuable and successful company.

In short, the cardinal principle in succession planning is to scrutinize the past 'wake' of the proposed candidate with greater rigour than only rely on performance metrics. Beware of competence without humanity or humility. Did the candidate deliver performance and earn people's respect without trampling all over? Directors can make serious enquiries and reflect on the admittedly subjective data.

After writing my book on lessons from the rise and exit of CEOs[5] and after reflecting on my 30 years sitting on Boards, I state the obvious: that the Board must be better accountable for CEO selection. While a nominations or selection committee may run a process and a headhunter may be appointed for the search, they do so *on behalf* of the Board, which is the decision-making authority. Hence, directors must engage directly with the headhunter/selection committee to engage with their views. They must get comfort from the final recommendation. In my experience this does not happen rigorously enough.

An MIT study of year 2000 suggested that CEOs appointed after 1985 are three times more likely to be fired than CEOs appointed before. It may well be a sign of changing times, but directors must reflect on the fuzzy ways of CEO selection.

---

[5]R Gopalakrishnan, *Crash: Lessons from the Entry and Exit of CEOs,* Penguin, 2019.

Directors do apply their mind, but they inadvertently abdicate their responsibility to the selection committee. When a CEO is fired, the board stays, which seems a tad unfair.

Here are five suggestions for bosses to consider:

i.   In promoter-driven companies and in PSUs, promoters who are not board members often communicate with the CEO, whereas they should have the discipline to express their views through their board nominees. Even though a director may be a promoter-nominee, the director will and should use judgment in accepting or modifying such views expressed. Multiple and contrary views can leave a new CEO quite flustered with contrary instructions.

ii. The board must collectively agree on a clear definition of the leadership skills sought from the CEO at that point of time. Boards most likely omit squishy leadership stuff like moving hearts, listening attentively and welcoming diversity. Inadequate discussion is devoted to culture fit, though they later realize cultural misfits! That a coordinated board is mandate for the CEO is not made explicit to the incoming CEO. CEOs are exhorted in a general way to provide a bold direction and to be their own man. When they do so, discomfort sets in. Consider what happened to Chris Viehbacher at Sanofi or Vikram Pandit at Citicorp, both of whom were discussed in *Crash*.

iii. Boards should delegate, not abdicate, to the search committee. Assuming an appropriate brief and work plan, they acquiesce, rather than engage, in the hiring decision—the search committee recommends, the board engages/approves. Directors are unaware of special conditions for the new CEO selection until much later. Which board accepts responsibility for failure of its judgment if the CEO appointment fails?

iv. Leaders are required to have people skills to move human hearts. This is a nebulous and soft subject. So, directors look for track record in market capitalization, product market share or profit growth. Many years ago, iconic Coco-Cola CEO Roberto Goizueta was succeeded by his CFO, Douglas Ivester. Alas, Ivester was a first-class financial whiz, but emotionally inept. The succession did not work out. The story of Richard Thoman at Xerox has similarities.

v. One-man initiatives and overpaying for acquisitions are the other factors in CEO firings. At General Electric, Jack Welch relentlessly drove an enormous finance business under one set of circumstances. Jeff Immelt could not do so in the dramatically changed market of the new millennium, and he wound it down. To bolster growth, Jeff Immelt acquired Alstom's power business in 2015 in a $10 billion deal. The acquisition not only failed to deliver target results, it resulted in write-offs and marking down of assets by $23 billion. Immelt's successor, John L. Flannery, faced the falling knives and was eased out in less than a year for not dealing with legacy issues. The Board stayed, but the CEO was eased out.

∽

The Culture of Questioning

When I initially proposed a wind energy proposal to the ITC Board of Directors in the late '80s, it was turned down on grounds of promising an inadequate internal rate of return (IRR).

Then an opportunity surfaced 20 years later. Wind energy as a proposition had made progress and the government was offering a package of incentives to encourage companies from the sector to invest. Feasibility had improved and the goal seemed within reach. Tamil Nadu appeared to be ahead among the states with almost 50 per cent of the wind energy capacity installed in the country. Since I was in Chennai at that time, I had good opportunities to hear success stories from others, visit wind sites and meet government authorities on the subject.

There were inevitable doubts and question marks in a large organization about the whole concept of wind energy and the statistical uncertainties of wind availability throughout the year. All projects were thoroughly checked by the finance department in Kolkata and proposals cross-checked for veracity and feasibility before being put up and circulated as a capital investment with good returns. This was a healthy check and balance on runaway ideas from the divisions of a diversified conglomerate. The enthusiasm and freedom to pursue divisional goals was encouraged by ITC's Board of Directors and the corporate management committee. Yet all divisional plans had to impartially pass the test of logic and had to stand up to the scrutiny of reliability in the forecast of returns.

A culture of asking and re-asking fundamental questions was encouraged and no question was too silly to be asked, such as:

♦ What is this investment all about and what will it do for ITC?

♦ Can you explain the technology in a layman's language? How will it be advantageous for ITC?

♦ Is it a proven technology, and if so, where? Can you cite examples?

♦ Can we handle such technologies with our current capabilities? Who would be responsible for maintenance?

♦ Who is the key supplier-manufacturer and what are the pros and cons of each player according to you? What guarantees do they give on performance?

♦ What are your assumptions in your profitability statement? On what basis? Is there a sensitivity analysis included of possible scenarios? What is the worst case and risk for ITC?

♦ How confident are you of the proposed returns and cash flow?

♦ Whom have you met to ensure and checkout continuity of government policies? The Electricity Board? Taxation assumptions? Depreciation assumptions? Carbon Credit assumptions?

- Are land assumptions and title deeds checked out? Can litigation take place at a later stage? What about security at these sites? What about environmental considerations and the probability of bird hits?
- How will these investments be managed in a steady state after the project is completed? How will you report back on an ongoing basis, especially when locations are far flung?

Since the subject cut across several businesses and functions, it was felt that a wide cross-section of managers needed to be called for a meeting to the head office in Kolkata to get some consensus over and cohesion of efforts. Wind turbine manufacturers were requested to make presentations right from the basic principles to get everybody on board. It tested the patience of the teams presenting proposals. Questions and 'what if' scenarios flew randomly over several hours. What appeared to be a chaotic process was making some headway slowly, after initial doubts and curiosities were satisfied. It was tiring and time consuming.

Over a number of these meetings, the consensus began to emerge that a trial could be launched in Tamil Nadu to test the concept. The packaging factory at Tiruvottiyur could put up a wind energy project of 14 MW for captive consumption. Two separate sites were chosen, at Theni and Kanyakumari, through Vestas and Suzlon, respectively. This was approved by the corporate management committee and the ITC Board of Directors, and a green signal given to the division to start and finish in record time. Over the next one year, the results were proved beyond doubt and there was a perceptible jump in confidence all around. By the time the next year's plans came around many other divisions/SBUs expressed interest in making similar investments in their states. In the next two–three years over 100 MW of wind energy was installed and clarity, consensus and negotiations improved at every round of investment thanks to learning from past experiences.

Organizational learning across functions and businesses and capex plans goes up incrementally when a process of freedom to ask questions and seek conviction is established as a culture. Across the organization, knowledge had moved up soberly with a clearer understanding of the essentials of wind turbines and wind energy, site selection based on wind mast data, changes in state laws and the ability and willingness of State Electricity Boards (SEBs) to evacuate the energy generated and feed it back into the grid. Over the next 10–20 years the data generated would be invaluable in planning the next lot of investments as the older turbines would need replacement either at their current locations or at alternative sites with better wind energy potential.

The sustainability efforts of the organization also received a boost as quantifiable data populated the progress path of renewable energy generated and carbon credits harnessed. This helped the overall goal of the organization to become carbon positive in climatic terms.

The culture of asking and re-asking fundamental questions was not restricted to wind energy. Any new investment and capital expenditure received the same treatment and process, making decisions more robust and sharing facts more transparent across the organization.

Safety, Health & Environment

Another example in a different area altogether can help to further illustrate the point. An emphasis on environment, health and safety was needed to dramatically alter the approach of the organization especially after Bhopal, Chernobyl and Exxon Valdez accidents. It was clear that ITC could not improve with workshops and exhortation alone. A formal structure was created giving EHS greater importance. Knowledge through experts was tapped aggressively and a close liaison created with safety organizations from whom we could learn more. DuPont was certainly an inspiring example. The safety manager in each division/SBU was given due importance and equipped further with a safety officer at each site. Inspection and audit were formalized, and the findings shared with the auditee team before finalizing the report. Tracking was established such that an accident anywhere would be automatically reported to Central EHS and the chairman was kept advised. Suggestions were invited to eliminate accident hazards and eliminate repetition.

The focus on prevention mobilized all managers at work and even beyond office hours, such as safe driving and the wearing of seat belts in cars and the wearing of safety helmets on two wheelers. Unhelpful beliefs and overconfident assertions gradually disappeared in the face of reality. A non-executive director of the Board was requested to take charge of the Audit Committee and visits organized for other non-executive directors of the Board to join him in reviews with each Division/SBU by rotation in each of its sites. Relevant accidents brought to their notice by the Central EHS Team ensured focus during these reviews. Visits were made to areas of the factory or office where the accidents had taken place to assess what could have been done by way of pre-emption.

It started working!

Accidents came down steadily and serious accidents plummeted. Smaller accidents then became the focus with 'near misses' given due importance. The culture was changing towards greater safety, with all managers required to undergo training irrespective of function. This was recorded and reflected in the appraisals of each individual. The entire table of awareness, knowledge and ownership had moved up across the organization.

∽

Remember Who You Are

There is an old saying that the higher the monkey climbs, the more you can see of his bottom. The person whom you knew as the young regional manager does not seem to be the same person that you see as the company director.

Such change happens not only to the person, but also to others' perception of the person. As we rise in our career, we must recognize this reality. The truth is that as senior leaders, we not only serve our company, but also act as stewards of the society we live in. We need not manipulate or influence this change, but we must remain authentic to who we really are.

'Authenticity is largely defined by what other people see in you and, as such, can to a great extent be controlled by you [...] Indeed managers who exercise no control over the expression of their authentic selves get into trouble very quickly when they move into leadership roles,' according to academics, Rob Goffee and Gareth Jones.[6]

---

[6]Rob Goffee and Gareth Jones, 'Managing Authenticity: The Paradox of Great Leadership', *Harvard Business Review*, December 2005, https://hbr.org/2005/12/managing-authenticity-the-paradox-of-great-leadership.

Whether you are a subordinate or a boss, a husband or a wife, a landlord or a tenant, whoever you may be, you would consider it a virtue to be perceived as authentic. The dictionary definition of authentic is 'conforming to fact and therefore worthy of trust, reliance or belief'. Its synonyms are listed as bona fide, genuine, real and undoubted.

There really is not much difference between the dictionary definition and the popular understanding. Everybody, just about anybody you can think of, thinks of the word authenticity in a similar way. But if this is the meaning, is it a virtue to speak out your mind in explicit terms all the time? Perhaps not. Life would be impossible if every person said or did what is really on their mind. For example, you would make an awful spouse if you were to share every thought or opinion exactly as you think or feel. It would be the same between a boss and a subordinate. In no human relationship can you communicate exactly what you feel.

So, does that make you inauthentic? You would not agree with such an assessment!

We associate authenticity with sincerity, honesty and integrity. We assume that it is an innate quality in every human being—that each individual either is authentic or is inauthentic. We assume that an authentic person is consistently so and conversely, inauthentic people are always so. Authenticity is thought of as the opposite of artifice, which means not straight-forward, sincere and uncomplicated.

This way of thinking about authenticity is flawed and is just not true. The reality is that your behaviour is a planned balance between expressing your personality and managing the impressions of those whom you wish to relate to. Yes, managing others, but that does not have to connote manipulativeness or untruthfulness. The yawning gap between the general imagery and the practice of authenticity causes dilemmas about behavioural ethics.

If you have had a bad experience with a person, you think of that person as unreliable and inauthentic. If someone else has had a good experience with the same person, he or she thinks the opposite. The person is the same, but the circumstance of the relationship determines whether the person is regarded as authentic or not.

I Am Who I Am

As a discipline and as self-instruction, I wrote down a sketch of who I am and what shaped me. It is not for me to judge whether my behaviour has always been consistent with who I am, that privilege belongs to former colleagues and friends.

Here is the sketch for what it is worth. Family and childhood background matter, but personal experiences matter more. Otherwise siblings would be similar. But they are not. It is very educative to contemplate your own life story, and better still, write it up. Your self-exercise will be of great value to yourself. You have yours as a distinctive story as I have mine.

I narrate mine here, not because it is exemplary or particularly interesting, but merely to illustrate how I remind myself of who I am. It may not be generally inspiring to recall who I am, but I do feel more aware of myself.

Both my parents were born in small villages in Tamil Nadu. One was called Vilakudi and the other was Gobi, and they were 400 kilometres apart. Neither of my parents could secure an education beyond school. My father devised an ingenious plan to leave the numbing atmosphere of his village and join his elder brother in the city of Kolkata, in order to seek a life of opportunity. Kolkata was quite a vibrant metropolis during the 1930s.

In due course, through determination and positivity, he worked his way up to acquire a professional accountancy qualification and rose impressively to become a senior departmental manager in a multinational company. My mother supported my father as a homemaker in the task of raising a large family.

As future events would show, both were quick learners and highly adaptive; they were savvy and smart. They adapted to the city ways and learnt how to advance and progress their economic and family life. But at heart, they were both village folks with simple values.

At home, we used to eat a traditional meal in a traditional way, after saying a prayer of thanks for the meal to follow. My father would shop astutely at the vegetable market every week to stock up (there was no refrigerator at home) and to keep in touch with the reality of household costs. My mother cooked initially, and remained closely involved with what was served on the table , even in her later years. Both would narrate the stories of village life and our grandparents. Our parents had ensured that we were well versed in the great epics, and that the lilts of the Carnatic music lessons for my sisters could positively influence our sensibilities—along with reading Shakespeare and the Bible at school.

My parents hugely emphasized on education, probably because neither of them could acquire a basic college degree. 'I want all my children to get a degree, and possibly a double degree,' my mother would say, often dreamily; the message was dinned into our tiny heads.

To her credit, each one of us did accomplish her desire. Her passion that her children study, was briefly threatened when my father had no regular job for four years. During that period, my parents stubbornly cut all expenses other than education, enabling my brother to go to England, my sister to stand first in her university degree and the rest of us younger kids to suffer no dilution in the education received. Bless my mother's soul that her grandchildren have done even better.

Father was generous in some ways (like helping indigent relatives financially) but was also very careful with expenditure in other ways (like taking exciting holiday breaks or dining out). He would despise any form of borrowing. Though he had never studied Shakespeare, he would lyrically quote 'Neither a borrower nor a lender be', as often as he could. 'Spend only from what you earn' and 'deserve before you desire' were two mottos he hammered into us.

In my professional career, I am generally averse to borrowing, and certainly opposed to excessive borrowing. Some of my colleagues think that I am conservative when it comes to finances. Maybe I am. But perhaps the attitude was fixed in me by what I experienced early at home.

Another influence on my young mind began when I joined college. When I started to stay in the college hostel, the Jesuit-in-charge offered me the opportunity to teach evening classes to underprivileged children of the locality. 'You are so fortunate to get the education you have got; can you spare some time to teach less lucky kids?' he asked. How could one refuse? I think I taught well. I certainly got great joy out of teaching; I used to think I was spreading hope. Over time I so dearly wanted others to have some of the privilege of the learning I had received. I learnt what it is to care and share through teaching.

During the end stages of my college degree, I seriously considered becoming a researcher and a teacher. The poor remuneration discouraged me. Finally, I found a way to earn through a business career but get the satisfaction of teaching through my spare-time activities.

I have continued some form of teaching right through my career. My HLL export department colleagues and I taught a foreign trade course at Bombay University in the 1980s when foreign trade was a non-event in India. Many years after my graduation, my teacher, the late Prof G.S. Sanyal, requested me to teach at the Vinod Gupta School of Management in the IIT campus, I took leave from work and camped at IIT to fulfil my promise to him. Even these days, I teach a credit course at B-schools, titled LWNT, standing for 'Learning What's Not Taught.'

It is perhaps the same satisfaction of sharing that has given me the motivation and energy to write this book, and my earlier 17 books. Yes, you read it right, 17 books.

I know that 90 per cent of those who buy books do not read the books. But I still write. Why? It is only because I feel I must do so.

∞

Success, Be Not Proud

 A thought in every manager's head is, 'I agree that we should be bold and outspoken, but is it practical to follow? Can an ordinary person really work with courage?' The argument in the head says, 'I need the job badly, so I cannot afford to be courageous and risk the loss of the job'. Since all of us do periodically experience such feelings, it is easy to empathize with those thoughts. What then is the way to reconcile these two apparently opposite things: an idea that appeals with an action that carries a big risk?

In your life and career, you cannot choose what will happen to you. What must happen will happen. But you can choose how to respond when whatever must happen to you happens—this has been emphasized in ancient Indian philosophy. Therefore, each of us has choices, and we must live with the consequences of the choice we have exercised. If you can do that and be mentally at peace, then maybe it is alright. Thereafter, you should not grumble about God or fate, or express destructive dissatisfaction with your condition, irrespective of whether you are a vice-president, a BPO executive or even a peon.

Vincent was a driver in Bangalore. He was exceptionally cheerful. Whether it was midnight duty or early morning duty, he was able, willing and infectiously enthusiastic. Once I apologized for imposing successive days of heavy work with long hours on him. He ended up narrating his story.

His father worked in a car garage in Mangalore. There were many mouths to feed in the family, yet his father insisted that he should study. Vincent was so infatuated by car mechanics, that he would loiter around the garage as a helper rather than complete his school homework. He told his father that he would like to become a driver rather than study.

His father was disappointed. 'You should study more. If something happens to me, who will take care of your sisters?' he often said. However, Vincent chose the option of indulging in his passion rather than continue with his studies. That is how he drifted into driving.

'But surely all these long hours must make you sometimes regret it,' I persisted.

'Not really. After all, I chose to become a driver, so why feel regret? Even if I do feel so sometimes, I have to dismiss it. And, sir, I do get paid overtime and that helps me dream of making my son an engineer. My father would be proud to see his grandson as an engineer,' Vincent replied in a matter-of-fact way.

Recently, Vincent called to announce his daughter's marriage. He chirped, 'Sir, incidentally, my son completed his graduation in mechanical engineering and is going to work in a software company. I am sharing my joy because you used to enquire. I wish my father was around. He would think well of his grandson.' Vincent took responsibility for his decision and learned to live with the consequences with great cheer.

∞

UNDERSTANDING
THE CONTEXT

Direction, Not Distance

 Many managers spend a lot of their working time thinking about how to accelerate their promotions, how to impress the boss more than their colleagues can and how to earn money faster. The management world is indeed very competitive. So you feel that time must be spent thinking through such matters and taking appropriate actions—quite correct, but only in part.

The question to ask is: should the aim in one's career be going far or going in the right direction? Ideally, of course, you should achieve both, but that is not easy.

If you watch club-level golfers, you will see the point. Some stand on the tee box with the longest club and whack the ball with the might of an ox. They are the ones who want to see the ball soar away with accelerating speed. A few seconds later, when they observe where the ball has landed, they curse and crib. The ball has perhaps been lost or has landed in a difficult spot from where it would be difficult to play the next shot. Other golfers take a measured approach of landing the ball on the fairway at a spot where they want it to land. For them, the next stroke is as important as this first tee shot.

Both are valid ways to play the game. If you are very talented, you may learn to do both i.e., go far as well as land where you want. Many club-level golfers never achieve this.

The purpose of a career is to utilize your potential fully because that alone can give you satisfaction and a sense of self-esteem. This is so whether you are a chairman or an assistant. It becomes possible to achieve such satisfaction when you are surrounded by friendship and trust, which are essential for accomplishing managerial tasks. Nobody can do a management job all by themselves, this is a well-accepted fact. It is the web of relationships and friendships that enable a manager to navigate the choppy waters that the ship of his career will constantly encounter.

There was a fine movie made by Frank Capra which I recall seeing when I was young. Starring James Stewart and Donna Reed, it was named *It's a Wonderful Life*. The story is about a man, who thinks he is a failure. So he prepares to commit suicide. An angel is sent to prevent his act and to rescue him. The angel finds that the man lacks self-esteem and hence he thinks that his friends and relations do not much care for him. The angel takes him in an invisible form to overhear what his friends and relations think of him. He is surprised that he seemed to be loved by them all and that he mattered to them. His own perception of his failures in his career and his business activities bothered them little, and their love for him was overwhelming. He feels blessed.

The moral of the film is that no man who has friends is a failure.

∽

Harnessing People Power

Crises in companies are inevitable. They come in cycles. In the absence of any significant threat or problem, complacency sets in and even 'normal' behaviour fails to manifest itself. The *International Herald Tribune* on 25 October 2004, reported a fascinating story about crocodiles imported into China from Thailand.

Crocodile meat is eaten in China. To make it affordable, the Chinese forestry department eliminated the steep duties on imported breeder crocodiles in the mid-1990s. CrocoPark, Guangzhou bought nearly 40,000 crocodiles from Thailand in 1997 and 1998, filling the holds of five chartered Boeing 747 cargo jets. It was an attractive commercial deal for the Chinese; the Asian financial crisis had made the Thai sellers panicky and crocodile prices collapsed.

The hope was that low wages and highly-skilled farmers, as well as the well-developed road and port infrastructure, would rapidly convert China into a competitive producer of crocodile meat, purses and other goods. The logic must have seemed impeccable.

What happened thereafter was that these crocodiles

experienced some difficulty in adapting to the cooler climate of China compared to that of Thailand. The male crocodiles started eating more in late autumn and early winter than they did in Thailand. They became so plump that they lost their sex drive when the mating season arrived in spring! Impotence, obesity, runny noses, all conspired to make the Chinese dream difficult to realize.

Here is another example. The Japanese have always loved fresh fish, but the waters close to Japan have not held much fish for decades. To feed the population, the fishing boats got bigger and went farther than ever. The farther the fishermen went, the longer it took them to bring in the fish. If the return trip took more than a few days, the fish were not fresh. The Japanese did not like the taste. To solve this problem, fishing companies installed freezers on their boats. They would catch the fish and freeze them at sea. Unfortunately, the consumer could taste the difference between fresh and frozen fish: the frozen fish fetched a lower price. So, fishing companies installed fish tanks on the ship. They would catch the fish and stuff them in the tanks.

After a little thrashing around, the fish stopped moving. They were dull and tired, but alive. Unfortunately, the Japanese could still taste the difference. They liked the taste of lively, fresh fish, not sluggish fish! Finally, they hit upon an idea.

They added a small shark to each tank. The shark did eat a few fish, but the rest of them were challenged and kept on the move by the shark. The Japanese consumer got the freshest fish.

Leadership in the Face of a Crisis

The most important action that leaders take when there is a crisis, is to rally people around the task. Leaders exude the message that the survival task needs every person to be on board. When the leader reaches out to people, the right-brained items get generated richly and get executed quickly. Here is an example from my HUL days. It illustrates a paradox that we strive hard to achieve comfort, free of threats to survival and growth. But the mere act of approaching that goal seems to produce a bunch of unintended consequences such as less growth, poorer instincts and less preparedness for a fuller life.

An example from the detergent market is worth mentioning. Capacity limitations were prevalent in the 1970s and 1980s, and Hindustan Lever was producing to its full licensed capacity. Its market entry was Surf, a high priced, top-of-the-line brand, selling to the consumer for ₹20 per kilogram. There were several lower priced detergents in the market, the most notable being Nirma.

In 1973, when I was responsible for detergent sales in the western region, I recall being asked to do a survey of 'an Ahmedabad-based small-scale manufacturer called Nirma.' I recall reporting with the naiveté of a novice that I could not quite comprehend its operation and cost structure. However, this company was doing big things in the Ahmedabad market and could easily replicate it in all of Gujarat.

Karsanbhai Patel had started making detergents in 1969 in the backyard of his home in Ahmedabad. He mixed the product by hand in a 100 square feet shed. He worked 18 hours a day. He himself procured raw materials, mixed them and then he went around shops selling the product. Since it was priced so low, he found he had a success on his hands. He moved to a bigger facility at Vatva, an industrial suburb of Ahmedabad. He branded it 'Nirma' after his daughter Nirupama. He targeted the poor localities and rural consumers, who would benefit from the low price.

The volume of the HLL brand Surf did not erode but the share of Surf eroded over 15 years from 1973 to 1987. Apart from some bluster and tactical responses, HLL felt it had limited options to respond to brands like Nirma that retailed at one-third the price of Surf. The limitation of options was due to a highly restrictive production environment imposed by the government's licensing system. If HLL responded through price cuts, it would reduce the profits per ton of limited licensed capacity. Developing new, low-cost brands would eat into the same limited capacity; anyway, the company had not been successful with such attempts. Outsourcing of production was not legally permitted as the company was considered a foreign company and had certain regulatory restrictions.

The consequence of all this was a steady erosion in market share (not necessarily of company profits), a huge irritation within the company with these 'snipers' like Nirma and a steady growth in these competitors' cash flow and brand success.

Around 1987, Chairman Ashok Ganguly felt that things had gone too far. At about this time, I joined the board as an exports director. I had no functional responsibility of detergents. It was run by two talented and experienced colleagues on the board, Susim Datta and Shunu Sen.

I recall my very first half-yearly board conference. I had conjured up this image of a wise and genteel group that would have esoteric discussions on long-term issues. Instead, Ashok Ganguly opened that meeting with a blunt and workman-like approach that puzzled me. Vice-Chairman Susim Datta and marketing director Shunu Sen had, what I thought, was a serious look on their faces. I heard urgency in Ashok Ganguly's voice. 'We are in deep trouble, gentlemen, and we have to get out of it because we are the guys who got into it. It is time for some plain speaking amongst us,' he said. There was just a plain admission of responsibility and a call for collective action. Quite a sobering start to a first meeting, many more of which I was to participate in, over the next few years.

What Ganguly was doing was to recognize the crayfish amidst the snails and ask all of us collectively to stop pretending that there was no problem.

He and Vice-Chairman Susim Datta redirected the company's rich resources and talent from developing, convincing excuses to finding aggressive solutions. A crack project team, code-named 'Sting', was set up to meet a challenging brief. It was, in hindsight, a terrific exercise in how leadership can redirect resources within a company to meet the needs of survival and growth, where it sees the threat as the biggest opportunity.

The birth and subsequent success of Wheel detergent bar and powder became a part of Unilever folklore in the next few years as Datta and Ganguly led the effort from the front. In the 1990s when Susim Datta was chairman, Gessy Lever extended the concept to Brazil as part of Unilever's efforts to spread best practices across the world. Wheel is perhaps still the single-largest brand in the Hindustan Lever portfolio.

Of course, Nirma too has gone from strength to strength, but in a somewhat different trajectory than earlier. New detergent brands entered the market at a price point even lower than Nirma's (they pulled a Nirma on Nirma!), causing the consumption market to prise open dramatically. Nirma made investments through integrating backwards: the company began to manufacture the raw materials required for detergent manufacture to strengthen its competitive position.

∽

 I was away on a business tour in Europe in 1996 along with a colleague when I heard the shocking news of the Enforcement Directorate in India arresting some of the directors of our company, ITC Ltd. My colleague and I struggled to cope with this disastrous news. We were incensed at the unfairness of it all. We had worked for over two decades with a company that we respected; we were proud of ITC's track record of tax and legal compliance. We felt that even if there was a dispute, it could be resolved across the table rather than the shock and awe tactics symptomatic of Foreign Exchange Regulation Act (FERA) days.

We completed our trip hurriedly and returned to India. The media had sensationalized the news. From the government's point of view, it was a search and seizure operation authorized by the law, irrespective of the status of the company or its directors. From our perspective, it was a blow to our pride and the people we had known, respected and worked with.

To add to our misery, news began to filter in of countrywide search operations and of being managers subjected to night-long interrogations and being threatened with dire consequences if they did not make confessional statements.

Nothing in life had prepared me for such an awful experience. ITC Ltd had professionals from every discipline. It prided itself on an open culture, with the freedom to disagree and to argue for what was in the best interest of the company's customers, shareholders, employees and society. Such humiliation was unwarranted to one of the highest taxpayers in the country and one of the highest foreign exchange earners, being a star exporter.

The magazine *India Today* carried banner headlines:

**'ITC in the Doldrums Following Raids,
Corruption Charges'[7]**

'With almost all its top brass in jail, or perilously close to it, it's difficult to see how ITC will handle the fallout of the $100 million FERA violation case.'

Outlook carried the following headline:

'ITC's Moment of Reckoning'[8]

'The government's brutal crackdown leaves corporate India shell-shocked.'

The purpose here is not to delve into a postmortem of these FERA raids and its aftermath and resolution. It is to reflect upon the experience of unanticipated shock and disappointment one felt at what was happening to normal, law-abiding people.

Sometimes experience steadily helps you gain confidence and skills. Sometimes experience hits you like a tidal wave, leaving you struggling to catch your breath.

At the core, is the ostensible issue or trigger and its genesis, growth and aftermath. There is volatility in the accusations made and in the inquiries following such dramatic raids. The media reports ball-by-ball but is caught up in the sensationalism of reputations taking a hit during a government crackdown. Personalities either distance themselves or make

---

[7]Navneet Sharma, 'ITC in the Doldrums Following Raids, Corruption Charges', 30 November 1996, *India Today*, https://www.indiatoday.in/magazine/economy/story/19961130-itc-in-the-doldrums-following-raids-corruption-charges-834114-1996-11-30.

[8]Arindam Mukherjee, 'ITC's Moment of Reckoning', 13 November 1996, *Outlook*, https://magazine.outlookindia.com/story/itcs-moment-of-reckoning/202502.

sweeping generalizations, like there is no smoke without fire.

Let's look at some of the learnings from the experience. At one level, the legal issues had to be managed. At another level, the company had to get back on its feet and restore balance to normal commercial activities for which it had been created in the first place. The largest shareholder, British American Tobacco (BAT), with 30 per cent, recommended that those who had been implicated should not continue to hold their portfolios and that their responsibilities needed to be redistributed.

An Interim Management Committee (IMC) was formed, in which I got an opportunity to play a corporate role, in addition to my responsibility as a divisional CEO. It opened a framework, giving me an opportunity to see the wider facets of the company's operations and legal issues to which I had not had the same exposure before. BAT insisted on participating in the IMC but the executive chairman, YC Deveshwar, insisted that this would be dysfunctional. Non-executive directors representing the overseas shareholder should not be taking on an executive role, negating the role of the ITC Board of Directors. BAT had often referred to the Cadbury Committee Report of 1992 on corporate governance.

Now they were caught up with their own inconsistency in seeking to participate in executive decision making. In most other countries of the world, they were operating subsidiaries and such interventions may have seemed natural and permissible for the largest shareholder. ITC was a different example of an associate company where they had a 30 per cent shareholding and had to work through the Board of Directors for better governance. BAT relented and stepped back to Board level participation in corporate governance. The immediate crisis was overcome without decision-making suffering in any manner, despite the overall stresses and strains of coping with legal enquiries and investigations and the glare of media publicity.

The IMC gave way to the Corporate Management Committee (CMC) consisting of executive directors and senior executives. This became the top executive decision-making body. At the very top, the Board of Directors consisting of executive directors balanced by non-executive directors took charge of corporate governance and strategic direction. Below the CMC, the Divisional Management Committees took charge of running their businesses competitively as SBUs responsible for profit, growth and survival.

In the post Enron situation after 2000–1 aspects of corporate governance got a further fillip in line with international developments on the subject. India's own national committees on corporate governance followed suit through various committees. In broad terms, one could appreciate the strengthening of the Audit Committee to cover new accounting standards and related party transactions being reported. The creation of the Nominations Committee and Remunerations Committee were other hallmarks. There was an overall balance sought on unchecked executive powers by increasing the number of non-executive directors of whom independent directors were designed to play an important part and protect minority shareholder interests. ITC grew in the process. And so did I.

I looked back at the events of 1996 and what followed thereafter in the larger context of better corporate governance. It made sense and made a strong impression on me to appreciate the eye of the eagle in as much as appreciating the view of the worm. There could be different ways of expressing these perspectives such as acquiring a helicopter view or being able to see the distant horizon now and then to avoid getting myopic. I had grown immeasurably in several ways following these experiences.

The net learning was dynamic, and I began to appreciate seeing things simultaneously at close range, mid-range and far into the distance. There are many instances where the micro affects the macro and vice-versa. I was invariably deeply immersed in one while trying to get an appreciation of the other two—often imperfectly or with blurred vision! Inevitably one or more images were frozen in time and no longer as accurate as before to enable the best decision. My grasp of the interdependent factors affecting success while coming out of adversity and initial setbacks changed dramatically.

In hindsight, I think ITC leadership managed to enlist both the emotional and physical energy of its large number of managers and staff. I will always remember the people power that the employees displayed at the time.

_ɔ∞_

Sleepwalking Doesn't Work

 The festive season and parties are going on. Lots of fun and a little less sleep over this week is understandable. However, as a general statement of lifestyle, inadequate sleep is a bad idea. It distracts you in a way which creeps up on you imperceptibly.

Young executives mistake sleeplessness with vitality and style. They proudly proclaim how long they work, how they need to socialize until late and how they manage with only five hours of sleep.

Then there is the bravado of self-importance about not being able to take a few days' leave. Taken together, you have a recipe for disaster—not merely to health, but to judgment.

Leonardo da Vinci wrote, 'Every now and then, take a little relaxation, because when you come back to work, your judgment will be surer. To remain constantly at work will cause you to lose your power of judgement.'

Harvard Medical School Professor Charles A. Czeisler is one of the world's leading authorities on human sleep cycles and the biology of sleep and wakefulness. He has observed that top executives have a critical responsibility to take sleeplessness seriously.[9] Sleep deprivation is not just an individual health hazard, it is a societal one.

Animals take short and quick catnaps, and do not require long stretches of sleep. It is different with humans. Although some are lucky to feel rested with catnaps, most people need more.

When you are drowsy, several thousand sleep neurons in the brain take over, and you involuntarily lose control. Sometimes it is for just a few seconds, but God forbid you're engaged in an activity that requires you to remain alert, for example, driving.

Pradeep was just 30 when he joined a large company as a mid-career recruit. He was well qualified, had gathered considerable experience in selling and was gregarious and relationship-oriented—all the ingredients that the company sought in its marketing people.

Pradeep enjoyed his drinks, parties and late nights. He was a hard worker. He was not only a natural business leader, but also a social leader. He would boast that his managers were colleagues at work, but in the evenings, they were friends—Anil, Arun, Anand, whatever. Being a competent person with strong people skills, Pradeep became a big hit all around.

His bosses appreciated his hard work and his ability to deliver results, his subordinates loved his open style. His peers grudgingly admired his ability to socialize endlessly, whereas they could not keep up. Pradeep quickly rose in the company. Within 10 years, he was pretty much at the top-leadership level of the company.

Progressively, he put on weight and started to slowdown perceptibly. It was never clear whether this was just the natural

[9]Bronwyn Fryer, 'Sleep Deficit: The Performance Killer', October 2006, *Harvard Business Review*, https://hbr.org/2006/10/sleep-deficit-the-performance-killer.

biological process or was accelerated by his lifestyle. Anyway, his energy was boundless, and it could mask any telltale signs. If he seemed a bit unfocussed occasionally, it was assumed that the previous night must have been a sleepless one, but he would be fine the following day.

By now, Pradeep was running a large division, and was taking big decisions. At precisely the time when his judgement was crucial for the business, it became erratic. He developed differences with his boss and he took new product decisions that went wrong. Several unexpected ailments started to plague the division. He resented it when these failings were pointed out, as he was convinced that he had a 'proven' track record. Finally, he quit to join another company. He was able to impress his new colleagues because of his social skills and positive demeanour. However, he made wrong judgement calls again, and had to change jobs again.

Habits are the key to success. You succeed by doing things right on a regular basis.

It is pointless to eulogize a leader who does without much sleep, or travels across time zones for extended time periods. You do not know when the sleep disorder syndrome will attack and become the performance killer.

∽

I am always amazed at those who claim that they hardly sleep or survive on four hours of sleep a day.

There are yogis and sanyasis who say their sleep is so restful and peaceful that they can manage with fewer hours of sleep, and there lies the secret to their freshness. Then there are politicians who claim they have cultivated the knack of catnaps while travelling and are able to manage with a few hours of sleep at night.

I envy all of them and admire and respect those who are more gifted than most of us. How can an organization plan on recruiting only those who have this characteristic and hope that they can continue with such strengths for a lifetime? The Armed Forces recruit some of the fittest people in society and train them for long hours of stress and strain under adversity. Yet they do not plan on continuing such a policy for a lifetime or even for a career span. They know the value of rest and recuperation and the need for balance.

Eight hours of sleep, for an adult, is a reasonable expectation. 95 per cent of people will fall under this average. Some may be better able to ward off sleep during an emergency or under stress. However even such people need to catch up on sleep and cannot manage long periods of sleep loss without loss of concentration and performance. Pilots and flying crews are mandated rest before taking off on another flight as a safety precaution.

Quality is defined as fitness for purpose by the guru W. Edwards Deming. This touches the heart of the subject for organizations that need good people as resources to drive competitiveness. Athletic fitness is not the goal in a commercial enterprise but fitness for purpose must include those who are stable and balanced in their attention to work and not volatile due to lack of sleep. Those getting into leadership positions affect many others and organizations must guard against them being erratic due to lack of fitness, arising from sleep deprivation.

Now let us examine the competing demand for bursts of energy and dedication, sometimes stretching for long hours. Any organization requires such energy to rise to an emergency or face a rare challenge or provide acceleration to a project reaching culmination.

I recall signing a Long-Term Agreement at ITC's factory in Tiruvottiyur in the late 1980s, and it was essential for the management negotiation team and the Union office-bearers to complete the nitty-gritty of the negotiations and documentation even if it meant working through the night. We had to meet the Joint Labour Commissioner in Chennai at 10.30 in the morning to complete the process of conciliation under the Industrial Disputes Act. We had all been on a hectic routine for the last three weeks and the agreement seemed near at hand for a final finish. At 2.30 a.m., a key manager of the personnel department said he was suffering from fatigue and needed to go and sleep. This seemed preposterous. However, I thought after some debate, that it may be pragmatic to set a time limit and agree that he would have to return by 5.30 a.m. latest. Meanwhile, the rest of us would roll out the copies and get signatures. He could read things afresh and point out proofing errors or conflicting sentences, if any. As things turned out, he returned in good time and everything went according to plan; we signed the paper before the Labour Department at the appointed hour.

The purpose of sharing this example is to highlight the need for bursts of energy in everyday situations. The context may be a SAP software being rolled out and 'going live' the next morning or an engineering breakdown of a major machine that requires 24-hour attention. Or a special launch requiring preparation of the market by flushing out older products and creating conditions for the new product to be placed for customers in a timely manner, without loss of continuity or mix-ups. Often, the last phase leading to culmination may take several days of intense work—with managers willing to abide by tough time targets even while coping with contingencies. This requires stamina to sustain long hours and teamwork without getting irritated.

Steady State and Sudden Bursts

This may seem the opposite of everything that was stated in the earlier part of this section. However, the reality of most organizations is that we need both steady-state energy and bursts of concentrated energy to get things done. The two are essential attributes required of every manager. The analogy of the fuel consumption of a motor car may offer some lessons. Driving at a steady speed ensures the least fuel consumption and energy usage. Yet the car will have to slow down over speed breakers and accelerate where there is less traffic to intelligently get to its destination in time. The brakes and gears must be in good condition to enable appropriate changes in speed.

Human beings are not machines but they too need rest, recuperation and cooling down after periods of activity. They need to engage with others where a team goal is involved and to learn to manage individually where they can control the immediate outcome. In many cases, these priorities may overlap and create pressures to conform to others, whose efforts are essential for task completion. The Lone Ranger can often be a threat to themselves and to others too.

In simplified terms, a cricket team chasing runs in the last few overs of a One-Day match will put its batsmen under pressure to cope with the run-rate required for victory. If the bowling is tight, then the batsmen may have to run faster and better, between wickets to take cheeky singles without getting run-out. The opportunity to win by hitting glorious sixes and fours will not be ignored but the risks may be high, considering the potential loss of a good batsman when several wickets are already down. All these parameters are clear, albeit, in varying degrees, to 50,000 spectators watching the match and millions watching the direct telecast of the match. The tail-end batsmen also know they are under tremendous pressure to rise to the occasion and the fielding team cannot be underestimated. It is likely to be a touch -and-go affair till the last ball.

This is not far removed from what organizations must do. The game here is more complex due to the lack of visibility and the unperceived interdependence of functions, departments and geographies. Communication fills these gaps to the best extent possible but cannot be as graphic and instantaneous as a stadium experience or the direct telecast of an ODI cricket match with scores and figures updated till the last ball bowled and replays showing the closeness of the last run-out. Yet, the parallels are similar as competitors battle it out for the customer's attention and seek to win the battle of the brands.

We need managers to be able to do both and to have the stamina to keep alternating between the two for a lifetime—and yet in overall good health and fitness. We cannot have them burning out after two episodic bursts of energy. They must, therefore, learn to recuperate by themselves and ensure fitness for purpose for the long term and know what they must do in the short term when explosive energy is required of them.

Those who prefer either one of the extremes are inflexible and have not learned to pace themselves depending upon the situational demands. Amongst them, the ones who get hooked onto bursts of energy and adrenalin can be dangerous, as short-termism becomes a habit and they are bored by the steady state. In positions of power and authority, they may even create situations of emergency to recreate short-term bursts of adrenalin to keep themselves going. This can be risky, and many team participants are going to burn out or tire easily or fall sick when they are required most for the major challenges ahead.

Those who make a virtue of losing sleep and managing on low sleep are acting 'macho' when such displays are not appropriate. These examples cannot be held up to others as role models either. Such managers cannot be relied upon as they can never operate in steady-state conditions and will ruin the equilibrium of an organization that paces itself sensibly to competitiveness.

In summation, ensure that you sleep and get rest regularly to sustain your fitness and alertness, and ensure that others around you do the same!

∽

Doing It Right Matters

Young managers are taught to think that they should 'take charge' of their career, that they should purposefully plan what they wish to be, what milestones they should achieve and by when. The reality is completely different. There are more factors that are out of your control than that are within. This does not mean that all planning is useless, but this does leave many managers in an anxious state.

Your career goal is *your* statement of intent and desire. The company you work for, the boss's judgement of your work, your seniors' views of your potential, the opportunity that develops in the wider economy—all these have a strong influence too. So, your own plan has only a limited influence.

Once you recognize this, and more importantly, accept this, you can start to do things right rather than merely do the right things. There is a difference.

Doing the right things means planning a desired outcome for each action or initiative. Doing things right means to stretch and do your best and leave the results to turn out the way they will.

Dave M. Cote was the chairman of a large American

corporation, Honeywell Inc. When I met him some time ago, he told me a story about his career.

He was a young accountant in GE several years ago. He was working three levels below the company CFO, who in turn reported to the legendary chairman, Jack Welch. One of Dave's tasks was to compile a statement of the company's forward projection of sales and profits by year, country and business unit.

It was a mass of numbers and young Dave could not imagine what use it could be to anyone. He enquired about its utility from his senior managers but was advised to do what he had been assigned. The statement had been produced for many years, so would he please continue?!

The chairman was trying to tear down the bureaucratic culture of a very traditional company. He had, as is well known, acquired the label, 'neutron' to symbolize his bombarding the company with his change agenda. One day, the chairman received this complex statement, showing the company's five-year projection of sales and profits.

The chairman was incensed, so he called for the young man, who was 'producing this rubbish'. A nervous Dave Cote appeared before him and was too awed to answer the obvious question. He was packed off with the statement 'that smart guys like you should not do this kind of thing.' Presumably, the CFO's department was roasted over the coals, and Dave received confirmatory instructions to stop the compilation soon thereafter.

Dave wondered why his seniors had brushed aside his question on the same matter and responded with logic and alacrity to the chairman's hollering! Perhaps you have had such an experience already in your workplace.

At a company reception a few months later, the chairman

was surrounded by his officers. He noticed young Dave lurking around. He summoned him and enquired whether he had stopped compiling that useless statement. One of the seniors present interjected to clarify that it was Dave who had asked questions about the futility of such a statement.

'But you never told me that,' said the surprised chairman. Dave looked shy and remained silent.

Some weeks later Dave's big boss, the CFO, gave Dave a double promotion and applauded his courage in not letting down his team under the chairman's pressure. Of course, Dave was very competent. To his surprise, this unplanned episode informed others of his character, which was not at all what he was trying to highlight. Character is such an intangible, yet important, part of a leader's qualities. Dave's career advanced in GE and he later went on to become the chairman of another company.

So, you should remember to do things right rather than only doing the right things. And while doing so, remember that character is at least as important as competence. The world has enough competent people, but not enough managers with character.

Passion, but with Caution

 Business leaders pursue audacious goals, like building the country's largest factory or buying the largest competitor. Managerial single-mindedness and passion can be positive and negative. Only the outcome establishes whether it was a folly or vision. How do you tell the difference before the outcome is known? Here is a story from history.

Montezuma ruled the wealthy Aztec Empire, which is modern-day Mexico. The Aztecs fervently believed that a strange-looking god would come some day and redeem them. In 1519, Spanish conqueror, Hernán Cortés, along with just 600 men, advanced rapidly into the heart of the empire with little opposition from the Aztec forces. Montezuma passionately believed that Cortes was indeed the strange god they had been waiting for. Thus, he ignored the many signals of the predator's real motives. Through this folly, the Aztec Empire was lost to the Spanish without even a fight! There can be modern-day Montezumas in the business world too.

I asked for the views of N.S. Raghavan, one of the Infosys founders, and now running his own innovation-promoting fund. He said he looked for 'purpose.' Purpose is a decision you make through thought and introspection; it is there through your own design and action. It is bigger than you. It gives meaning to everything that you do. Arvind Chudasama of Okhamandal, Gujarat, illustrates this.

Tata Chemicals Rural Development Society (TCRDS) had assisted Arvind with a bank loan to buy a kulfi machine and deep freezer; Arvind had sensed that there was a market. His kulfi was liked and the deep freezer kept the kulfi intact during erratic electricity supplies. However, the season for kulfi was short, so Arvind had difficulty running his modest business.

'*Izzat ka sawal ho gaya*,' Arvind said. He just had to solve two problems: first, to pay off the loan as planned and second, to earn a decent living through his business. He was fed up of being poor. So he decided to seek a second loan from the bank, this time to buy a *chakda*—a motorcycle taxi that runs like a local bus service.

His family condemned it as an utterly foolish idea—he was sinking further to repay the first debt. However, the TCSRD officers saw a glint in Arvind's eye, what one might call 'purpose'. He spoke passionately about getting his family out of the cycle of poverty by learning to do new things, which would generate income for him. He would run the chakda and earn enough to repay the chakda loan, use it for effectively selling kulfi during season, use the deep freezer to support selling of dairy products throughout the year; he would make a business of both. It was an audacious idea.

TCSRD officers said, 'He was set on achieving something bigger than himself: getting his family out of poverty. He was young, determined and he had a sort of light in his eye. He was single-minded about overcoming the obstacles.' The bank took the risk.

The outcome of whether the family will emerge from the

poverty cycle is still not known. But so far, he is returning the instalments on both the kulfi machine and the chakda. He has plans of taking another loan to buy a generator and a cold drink-making machine for the manufacture and sale of different flavored aerated drinks.

Because he has a purpose, it is more likely than not, that in the future, he will be thought of by his family and society as a visionary and not a fool. But it will be some time before that can be confirmed!

∽

Passionate managers can help burn new trails in an organization and help change the status quo towards a higher level of performance and achievement. Consider a Bob Beamon breaking the triple jump record or an Usain Bolt creating a fresh 100 metre record under 10 seconds! Can such athletic prowess have relevance to organizations?

Mihaly Csikszentmihalyi is a Hungarian-American psychologist who wrote about the concept of flow in his book in 1975.[10] Almost everyone has experienced this state of productive flow when one's energies and concentration are focused exclusively on a single subject or task to the exclusion of everything else. A child is engaged in a task of building blocks and seems to be enjoying himself, oblivious to distractions.

People often refer to a state providing an energy of its own as exemplified by an artiste absorbed in music. Or a scientist absorbed in a complex problem. Or a writer hitting a train of

---

[10]Mihaly Csikszentmihalyi, *Beyond Boredom and Anxiety: Experiencing Flow in Work and Play*, Jossey-Bass Publishers, 1975.

thought that carries him forward with its own momentum. Or a sportsman settled at the batting crease and engaged in batting well without getting distracted by catcalls or applause from the gallery.

If the task is too easy, then there is a loss of concentration as one's full faculties have not been mobilized to the cause. If the task appears too difficult, the concentration flags again. The best results flow when the challenge seems difficult and yet not totally out of reach, demanding the best from the participant. The parameters may change continuously in a dynamic way. A person playing a computer game may be an example of creative absorption in winning, often willing to forego food, drink and sleep!

Passionate managers often seem crazy in their espousal and determination to launch a new product or open a new market or introduce a leapfrog technology or innovation in finance or human resource management or in any discipline for that matter. They bring extraordinary enthusiasm and persistence to their efforts, sometimes exasperating colleagues and others in the process. Clearly, they are in some state of flow and displaying energy and determination to persist with their ideas until success is achieved. In the process, they may appear to ride roughshod over objections and others' feelings and opinions. They may be impatient with warnings of caution expressed by people around them.

How can an organization cope with this phenomenon and yet harness such energies for breakthrough and continuous improvement?

Passionate managers play an invaluable part in taking the lead initiative. They risk themselves and their reputation by espousing a stand or idea and do their best to achieve goals in that direction. They are the 'change champions', leading the way, and often need a sponsor or senior manager to broadly support them and their cause. This may or may not be their immediate boss. The organization needs to help build a project team around such a change champion and help organize meetings, reviews and record tracking in a meaningful way. This is more than a demarcation of space to meet along with some infrastructure and rules of communication. The team must cognize for who else could be the stakeholders and who else needs to know what is going on and what changes are likely to take place in the future. The team must develop skills in learning to work together, even as they improve skills in communication across boundaries.

Since facilitation through passion is an evolutionary process, others in the system may perceive the passionate change champions as overambitious, too visionary and impractical, lacking finesse and communication skills or downright foolish in their approach. This may change from time to time. Corrections and small adjustments are taking place constantly in individuals, the project team and the larger team. Some facilitation, by way of skill building and process work may be helpful. Too much, may derail the process. Too little, may allow the process to abort itself. There are principles of flow even in this facilitation!

The danger of labels is that they come with a baggage of history and people already have perceptions about them. Dr J.M. Juran, a contemporary of W. Edwards Deming, would have been able to embrace everything under his broad trilogy of Quality Planning, Quality Improvement and Quality Control.[11]

We do not want to get caught in labels or in a debate about

---

[11]Dr Joseph A DeFeo, 'The Juran Trilogy: Quality Planning', *Juran*, 15 April 2019, https://www.juran.com/blog/the-juran-trilogy-quality-planning/.

the Japanese contributions vis-à-vis the American Quality gurus. Every idea or tool has its virtues and we do not have to get caught in the semantics.

The challenge is to tap and mobilize the passion of individual managers while retaining the organization's stability and dependability for all its stakeholders. Sparks are required, otherwise there would be no improvement or innovation. The organization can learn to become smarter in mobilizing such energies without becoming unstable itself. It knows that unchanging stability is a path to ruin and decay.

Efforts Gone in Vain

As a young engineer at ITC's Saharanpur factory in the '70s, I was involved closely with a project with Molins of India to hybridize an older cigarette making machine, Mark5, with the design advantages of the new Molins Mark 8 cigarette maker. This was called the 5-8-5 project and would save the company crores of rupees in capital expenditure in an era of import restrictions. I plunged into the project with great enthusiasm even as several colleagues and seniors advised me of its futility and the likelihood of a Frankenstein. We succeeded partly in improving speed and the weight control system, although the hybrid could never be as cohesively designed as the modern Mark 8.

When test trials started, I volunteered to be an operator on the prototype machine to demonstrate its success, for three months. It took the life out of me, but the prototype worked, and I personally felt good! More machines were ordered and went into the system. Government policies, meanwhile, unexpectedly changed and imports became possible, eliminating the need for a hybrid. In retrospect, my efforts of over two years seemed to have been in vain or even foolish, although the interim period had been managed for the organization until policies changed for capital goods. I was left with pangs of doubt at having wasted two years on a project that had to be aborted eventually and would be written off the books. It required an understanding boss to explain to me that nothing had been foolishly wasted and that I had gained from the experience and so had the organization, although priorities had altered for genuine reasons.

Achievements tend to occur when a person's body or mind is stretched to its limits, in a voluntary effort to accomplish something that is difficult or worthwhile. This happens when we are focused on realistic goals with our skills matching the opportunities for action. Goals allow people to concentrate on the task at hand, forgetting other things temporarily. The key element of an optimal experience is that it is an end. The activity becomes intrinsically rewarding.

When a person is doing something voluntarily, concentration is accompanied by positive moods; when the activity is perceived to be forced, the correlation is negative.

Passionate managers may appear visionary and foolish at times but they bring voluntary energy to the task. Their enthusiasm can be infectious if the organization is able to channel their energies in a constructive way. Keeping them motivated sometimes against difficult odds requires a different approach from higher management.

I recall a spirited manager working at ITC's factory in Munger, Bihar, in the early '90s, wanting to implement the ISO 9000 Quality Standard. It seemed an impossible task, considering the cultural milieu of the place as ITC's oldest factory. The Union was not motivated and distanced itself from responsibility. The president was, however, open to the idea that it was a positive step. Raju, the Works Manager, felt passionately that he would like to give it a go. With a little support from me, he embarked upon the challenge with great enthusiasm and soon had the place warming to the task, albeit, with many small obstacles. He persisted.

The day came when the factory was to be officially certified, having passed all the tests and audits. The trade union president, Ram Badhan Rai, made a rousing speech to the workmen that they now had an AK-47 in their hands with ISO 9000 and need never look back with weakness! I was on the dais and looked shocked and whispered to him that this was a dangerous reference and not our intention at all. He smiled graciously in apology and said the people of Bihar would understand his language well and there was no harm in driving home dramatically that ISO 9000 was now a part of their competitive strategy!

∞

Virtues of Incremental Learning

The Quality Revolution enraptured me as I read about Deming and Juran helping Japan change after WW II and its aftermath. Across Total Quality Management (TQM) and Total Productive Maintenance (TPM) many initiatives were spawned, each with its own discipline and methodology of implementation, including the use of statistics on a scale never seen before.

My purpose here is not to trace historical evolution as much as to learn from these outstanding thinkers of the twenty-first century. The initial thrust was product quality, which went on to ensure process quality and then the robustness of design and the value of continuously improving the knowledge, skills and quality of all personnel and managerial processes across functions and departmental silos.

At the heart is Juran's Quality Trilogy of Quality Control, Quality Planning and Quality Improvement. Juran covers 'Breakthrough Improvement' to new performance levels and 'Continuous Improvement' to refine the processes further and quality control to hold the gains of such efforts. He states emphatically that such improvement takes place project by project and in no other way. This may seem bold and exclusive as stated but seems practical and sensible on reflection.

A sports example can lighten our reading and illustrate the point being made.

A twist service in tennis requires a certain approach and technique that cannot be learned by doing more of what one was doing earlier. It requires a new method and stance to be observed, adopted and practised until repeatable to an acceptable degree. Once a threshold of proficiency is achieved, various smaller improvements can be made to improve the ball toss, improve accuracy and vary pace and spin. Measurements need to be designed to track progress. The inclination to quit practice surfaces every now and then. Martina Navratilova mentions a small change in footwork and stance that altered her service in a major way.

A project-by-project approach works. This involves some sacrifice in the initial learning phase where progress is halting and fretful as new habits and insights get absorbed. Like learning how to drive a car, a series of trial and error experiences take a place even after demonstrations have been given and explained. This explains what happens at the individual level where somebody accepts the need to learn and practise a new method and approach.

What happens in an organization where there are many people? Each person is characterized by a unique tuning-fork frequency.

Group phenomenon comes into play for project-by-project improvement where several individuals are involved. Juran suggests the identification of potential projects and then making some choices on what to concentrate on depending upon business priorities. Thereafter, a sharper definition of the problem statement on the likely impact emerges. This can enable all team members to get on board. The data gathering and diagnostic journey may seem tiresome and teams may depreciate their importance. This can however be a costly mistake. The moment a clear goal emerges there is team clarity, which is different from an individual's clarity.

Group members are different human beings who bring their own biases and impatience and motivations to the group. A quick recap of an Ishikawa/Fishbone Diagram—named after Kauru Ishikawa, it is a cause and effect diagram used in quality circles to improve product design and prevent defects—helps catch up from wherever the team left off last. The team members acquire an identity of their own like a super-individual held together by a common objective.

In due course, a breakthrough improvement takes place, and this is formalized into a solution to reap benefits and hold onto the gains. Training of new recruits in the new methodology and knowledge becomes critical to prevent slippage. Finally, the gains of breakthrough improvement are locked into place.

A Quality Council or Steering Committee aided by a TQM Coordinator and Finance Staff track and monitor progress to harness the gains. These structures or labels are not the end goals. Measurement must take place to track progress systematically.

At ITC's Packaging & Printing Division in Chennai, I had an opportunity of launching the Juran Quality Improvement Projects with the help of Mr Suresh Lulla of Qimpro Consultants and got the International Quality Rating System (IQRS) into place with his assistance. Krish Chary took over as the TQM Manager. Mr Sunil Banerjee of Synergy Consultants had helped us earlier with the Zero-Defect Campaign (ZDC) at the shop floor level of both factories on which was built our ISO 9000 certifications. These initiatives led on to the IQRS of DNV based on a mix of the Malcolm Baldrige, European Federation of Quality Management (EFQM) and Deming criteria. Mr Krishna Kumar of DNV and his team were of enormous help. We were able to get the Munger and Tiruvottiyur factories and Divisional HQ audited by and certified to the IQRS scale moving up gradually over a period of time to between IQRS 6 to IQRS 8 on a scale of 10.

Excellence is a process of evolution, working through cumulative learning and thousands of small improvements.

This is a continuous journey as the goals are not frozen and keep shifting with business imperatives and competition and progress on other fronts. A new technology or a new MIS system such as SAP will cause a temporary spike/dip in the system before it settles down to a new equilibrium. Excellence is a process of evolution, cumulative learning and continuous improvement.

∽

Persistence Pays Dividends

 ITC Ltd promoted Bhadrachalam Paperboards Ltd as a separate company and as its diversification into the core sector of the economy in the late '70s. This worked out well. K.L. Chugh was deputed as a capable engineer to establish the project in a backward area in Khammam District, Andhra Pradesh. He reported to R.C. Sarin, the deputy chairman of ITC Ltd. Later in 1991, he took over as chairman of ITC Ltd from J.N. Sapru.

The objective of a suitable alternative supply for duplex boards was achieved and likewise ITC's diversification into a 'core sector' of the Indian economy—paper industry in a backward area. It was a commendable effort executed with dedicated professionalism in a remote area with indigenous tree plantation and research built into the value chain from the beginning.

I moved to the Packaging Division of ITC Ltd in Munger after having worked in the Tobacco Division for five years. The major trials on Bhadrachalam duplex board took place successfully at Munger during that period. We had been using Rohtas Board from Dalmianagar till then. Suddenly Rohtas closed permanently due to a combination of labour and financial problems. ITC's timely diversification into paperboards paid off in protecting its businesses. While stiffness was a desirable factor, the initial lots of paperboard from Bhadrachalam were too stiff and caused difficulties in cutting and creasing which, in turn, affected the performance of the downstream packing machines in the cigarette factories. This was overcome with a fast feedback loop set up between the packaging and printing factories and the paperboard mill. Quality stabilized quickly.

The market meanwhile, in the next 10 years, was gradually changing to coated boards. Better graphics and better value addition became important and the issue came to a head by 1994, a few years after India's economy had opened up post liberalization. In the vocabulary of papermakers, the decision was a toss-up between rebuilding Paper Machine-1 (PM-1) to produce coated board or buying a new machine (PM-4) with the right configuration and inline clay coating. Obviously, there would be a difference in costs.

The agony of a shutdown of PM-1 during the rebuild period with impacts on the market being managed in the interim, could not be underestimated either. A new machine, on the other hand, would have a modern headbox and a better wire configuration for folding box boards with better control over process parameters and better speeds with correspondingly faster drying. It was decided, after much debate, to go for a new machine equipped with the best in technology from Valmet and other international partners in paperboard manufacture.

My intention here is not to exhaust the reader with a primer on paper-making or chemical engineering. A new paperboard machine, depending upon its configuration, could cost ₹750–1000 crore and would take at least 18 months to erect and commission and at least one year to stabilize. It would have backward and forward linkages to be considered and complex logistics. Decisions must be taken reasonably in advance. Yet investing too far ahead of the evolving market could impact profitability adversely.

The challenge in 1996–97 when I joined the Bhadrachalam Board of Directors was to help stabilize PM-4 for cigarette packaging coated board requirements. The old shell and slide cigarette packs were undergoing a change to flip-top cartons. The cigarette business was bringing in modern cigarette packers from Focke and GD running at much higher speeds.

To cope with this, the packaging factories had to produce flip-top carton blanks of the right quality that would not compromise the efficiency of the packers. It was an immense change in packaging formats. Backward integrating further, the paperboard mill needed to produce a quality that could run on these modern print machines and be suitable for die cutting inline at high speeds. These printed carton blanks needed to run on the cigarette packers at high speeds with folds and tucks taking place to perfection. It was a period of major change and I was anxious to manage the changes smoothly.

Cascading Waterfall

Imagine a big change in the Niagara waterfalls getting transmitted throughout the passage of the water as it flows downstream.

Dr Bhima Sastri had come back to India for a short while, from the Westvaco Paper Mill, USA, and helped the team of Pradeep Dhobale, CEO and Sanjay Singh, Chief of Operations and K. Viswanathan, Head of Marketing, on improving quality to meet customer requirements. He frequently travelled the full distance from the paper mill to the packaging factory to the cigarette factory with me, to experience what was happening to changes made in the waterfall.

We conducted several hundred experiments and struggled upstream and downstream to stabilize the flow for the best operating parameters. At one point of time, the paperboard was printing all right but not responding so well to inline precision rotary die cutting. We had to go back to paperboard inputs to strike the right balance between softwood pulp and hardwood pulp and the right mix between short and long fibers.

At another point of time, the chalk loaded on the paperboard coating was excessive. The packer technicians at the cigarette factories pointed out the white dust settling on their machines and their moustaches as the new lots of paperboard blanks traversed their machines! We had to go back and reduce the chalk content by trial and error.

Technological changes of a major nature were taking place in the entire value chain in a dynamic context—at the paperboard stage, at the printing and packaging stage and at the cigarette packer stage and finally at the consumer end where it had to have international appeal and functionality. There were professionally qualified people at every station along this value chain that was changing along some parameter or the other but still required stable and steady responses to the end consumer. There were innumerable iterations and experiments to cope with changes in quality expectations at every stage. Each took its own time to settle down. It was a giant control system that stretched from tree-logging operations, all the way to the final consumer who was relatively unaware of what went into the product he was holding in his hand but frank in expressing his customer opinions and preferences. Like any control system, a small transient could affect and perturb the system disproportionately. Life could be hell until the system was brought back into a steady-state condition.

The impression people have is that scientific systems will work perfectly from the start. That is certainly every engineer's endeavour. However, we are working with materials (sometimes agricultural) and human elements all the time and there are variations along the value chain. Communication at a time of rapid change needs to be far better than during steady-state conditions, as interdependencies are not clear from the start. Pressure points change along the route as well. Results flow from experimentation done and these need to be studied against expectations. Often there are surprises and some unintended consequences too.

Better control systems helped management design better controls and feedback. Superior technology helped management improve reliability and speeds. Truth be told, management remains a performing art and not a predictable science.

As I look back, up and down the value chain, there were moments when the papermakers felt helpless and were getting stuck. They wrung their hands in anguish at the plateau they seemed to have struck. At other times, I recall anger and annoyance at our cigarette factories as new packers arrived on their shop floor and they were expected to commission machines quickly and the packing materials they had received seemed to be a bottleneck.

The packaging division was like an accordion between two larger divisions coping with its own changes and dealing with simultaneous changes at both ends of the spectrum. G.M.K. Raju, the CEO, and R. Senguttuvan, chief of operations, and the team did their best to maintain equilibrium even while coping innovatively with the big changes upstream and downstream.

They crafted marketing desires into superior graphics and functionality that could embrace both ends of the value chain.

During this entire period, nobody in the chain could be let off the hook for not meeting profit targets or not fulfilling their commitments to the Board on results. It was a splendid achievement.

At a macro level, the Board of ITC Ltd took a decision to absorb Bhadrachalam Paperboards into ITC and create a Paperboards and Specialty Papers Division. This also helped the cash flow of the paperboards and specialty papers business at a time of technology infusion and quality improvement. It paved the way for the acquisition of the Ballarpur paperboard mill at Kovai making recycled paperboards. Safety and environmental standards and quality standards improved significantly in all the units of the business.

I once took a helicopter ride from Hyderabad to Bhadrachalam. From a height, the waters of the Godavari seemed calm and unperturbed. As we came down, I saw the Godavari in its awesome breadth and then saw the waters choppy in parts, which I had not noticed earlier from a height. My heart missed a beat. I then imagined a human being clinging to a log of wood smashed away from his house during the floods when the Godavari was in spate, as it often happens during the monsoons.

I was humbled to consider that management is a performing art despite our advances in science. We will always require capable managers to constantly traverse perspectives at different heights and recalibrate what needs to be done at the right time intervals to ensure the best results.

Managing people and things in fine balance—in dynamic conditions—is truly a performing art despite advances in science.

they create marketing leaves my superior graphical and conceptually that each of these bath each of the wide chair. During this extra period, notably, in the plant Budh bat to fit the look for not meeting profit they feel for the time their contribution site the level or result. It was a splendid achievement.

Paper work is the speciality but as Obc 50t. This also helped the analog of the relationships and security report business. a major technology integration and quality in pressure work paved

Accepting a Different Approach

 Growing up in Kolkata, at one point of time, the family lived at an address called 9, Elgin Road. I was only seven years of age but would hear inspiring stories about the exploits of an Independence-era leader, who used to live opposite our house: Netaji Subhas Chandra Bose.

Netaji had begged to differ from Gandhiji's policies in the Congress party and quit the party to strike a more revolutionary path. He had been driven out of the house opposite to mine, by his nephew, in an Audi Wanderer, number plated BLA 7169, in 1941. In 1945, Netaji died in a plane crash, just seven years before we came to live at 9, Elgin Road. The bottom line of the narrative was that when he suffered pangs of conscience to accept the decisions and the approach of the Congress party, he quit to chart his own path. He could not accept those decisions from his superiors.

Much later, during my corporate career, I encountered situations of having to accept or protest decisions of a superior. In the face of a prevalent view in an environment, how can a manager think about his position? This is a common situation in leadership.

A person may express differences against a prevalent view among seniors because of four underlying reasons:

1. Difference of opinion (I disagree with your opinion).
2. Assertion of ego (I am right, and I would not like to be seen to be yielding to your view).
3. Matter of principle (I am unable to support this based on a principle).
4. Question of ethics (I don't support it because there seems to be financial wrongdoing).

A study of mythology, history and business is interesting and instructive. The driver for the difference ranges from a simple difference of opinion to one involving financial impropriety. Netaji quit Congress because of point (3) above. Nobody, who is involved, admits to the existence of point (2). The case below allowed me to think about the most common difference of opinion, which is of variety (1).

I set out to research the case.

Hyderabad Police Action

This story demonstrates the courage of General Bucher, speaking up at the right time and in accepting a different decision from his recommendation.

India became independent on 15 August 1947. Those were tumultuous times for the nation. Right after independence, Kashmir suffered infiltration from across the new border with Pakistan. A war between India and Pakistan over Kashmir began on 22 October 1947. At about the same time, problems brewed in the princely state of Hyderabad. Events unfolded simultaneously in Kashmir and Hyderabad.

The state of Hyderabad is located over most of India's

Deccan plateau. The dynasty and kingdom were established in 1724 by Asaf Jah after the collapse of the Moghul Empire. By the time of Independence, Hyderabad was the largest in area among all the 565 princely states, and the wealthiest by far. It had its own army, airline, telecommunications network, railways, postal system, radio broadcasting service and currency. Hyderabad's ruler was the Nizam, a Muslim, while most of the subject population was Hindu (85 per cent were Hindu and 12 per cent Muslim as per the 1941 census).

Since the beginning of the twentieth century, the state had started to become increasingly theocratic. In 1926, a retired Hyderabad official, Mahmud Nawaz Khan, founded the Ittehad (also known as MIM). Its objective was to unite the Muslims in the state in support of the Nizam and to reduce the Hindu majority by large-scale conversion to Islam. Ittehad emerged as a powerful communal organization, one that marginalized the political aspirations of the Hindu and the moderate Muslim population.

It is from this organization that Qasim Razwi emerged when the Nizam felt threatened by the events surrounding Indian independence. With the Nizam's tacit approval, Qasim Razvi put together a volunteer militia of Muslims; this came to be known as the Razakars.

In 1947, when Sardar Vallabhbhai Patel approached Hyderabad to sign the instrument of accession, the Nizam refused. He declared Hyderabad an independent state even though it was in the heart of India. When Patel requested the help of the English Governor General, Lord Mountbatten, he was advised to resolve the issue without the use of force. Accordingly, the Indian government offered Hyderabad a 'Standstill Agreement', which assured that the status quo would be maintained and negotiations could continue. Lord

Mountbatten himself presided over the negotiations and several possible deals were developed but were all rejected by the Hyderabad government.

There was considerable turmoil and unrest developing in Hyderabad right after independence. On 4 December 1947, a Hindu leader, Narayan Rao Pawar, made a failed attempt to assassinate the Nizam. The Nizam had nurtured a large army, with mercenaries hired from among Arabs, Rohillas and Pathans. The army was commanded by an Arab, Major General Syed Ahmed El Edroos.

Even as India and Hyderabad negotiated through 1948, the Nizam tacitly encouraged the Razakars to escalate the violence between them and the Hindu community. Muslim leaders are said to have made inflammatory statements and there is evidence of violence against the Hindu population.[12]

By March 1948, Lord Mountbatten heard rumours of an Indian plan called Operation Polo to move Indian troops into Hyderabad. He sent for the British commander-in-chief of the Indian Army, General Roy Bucher, to enquire what Polo was about. Bucher stated that he knew nothing about it. Later, after an enquiry, he clarified that it was the Indian government's contingency plan should a massacre of Hindus occur in Hyderabad.

In June 1948, Lord Mountbatten prepared the 'heads of agreement' deal, which offered Hyderabad the status of an autonomous dominion nation under India. The deal called for the restriction of the regular Hyderabad armed forces along with the disbanding of the militant Razakars. The Nizam would continue to be the executive head of the state pending plebiscite and elections. This plan, too, was rejected by the

---

[12]Mike Thompson, 'Hyderabad 1948: India's Hidden Massacre', *BBC*, 24 September 2013, https://www.bbc.com/news/magazine-24159594.

Nizam. Let alone signing an agreement, the Nizam issued a *firman*, an order, on 12 June 1947, demanding complete independence from India.

Patel was progressively getting tired of the Nizam's actions and wanted to put a quick end to the deteriorating string of developments. Patel wondered, 'How can the belly breathe if it is cut off from the main body?'[13] The civil law and order situation in Hyderabad was deteriorating fast, thanks to the activities of the Razakars. Patel told Lord Mountbatten, 'The Nizam has mortgaged his future to his own Frankenstein, the Ittehad.'[14]

Patel summoned Major Gen Chaudhuri, the Army chief in southern India, to assess his confidence and preparedness if the plans to enter Hyderabad were to be implemented. It was V.K. Krishna Menon, the Indian high commissioner in London, who suggested the terminology 'police action' rather than army action, even though it was clearly an army action. For such a plan to be implemented, cabinet sanction was essential. Jawaharlal Nehru was most reluctant, and Patel actually walked out of one cabinet meeting in protest. Nehru was jolted out of his complacency and started to relent. But he was under the contrary influence of Bucher, who was hesitant throughout the planning. Bucher overestimated the capacity of the Hyderabad army and underestimated that of his own troops.

A cabinet meeting was organized on 12 September 1948, to take a final decision. Among those who attended were Nehru, Patel, Baldev Singh, the defense minister, General Bucher, Air

---

[13]Sunil Purushotam, *From Raj to Republic: Sovereignty, Violence, and Democracy in India*, Stanford University Press, 2021.

[14]Durga Das, *Sardar Patel's Correspondence, 1945–50, Volume VII, Integrating Indian States—Police Action in Hyderabad*, Navjivan Publishing House; First edition, 1973.

Force Chief Air Marshall Sir Thomas Elmhurst and Lt Gen. K.M. Cariappa. As the decision to begin the Hyderabad police action got crystallized, General Bucher stood up and said, 'Gentlemen, you have taken a decision in a difficult matter. I must give you my warning. We are also committed to Kashmir. We cannot say how long it will take, so we will end up having two operations on our hands. This is not advisable, so as your commander in chief I ask you not to start the operations.'[15]

It was an act of great courage that the general spoke up clearly when it was required. General Bucher offered his resignation if his advice was not heeded. There was silence while a distressed and worried Nehru looked around. Patel interjected at this point: 'You may resign, General Bucher, but the police action will start tomorrow.'[16] A disappointed General Bucher left the room. The Hyderabad police action began the next day, on 13 September. Within five days the Nizam's forces were routed. By 4.00 p.m. on 17 September, Maj Gen Syed Ahmed El Edroos surrendered to the Indian Army's Maj Gen J.N. Chaudhuri in Secunderabad.

The leaders in India and Pakistan were both new to their national roles and somewhat inexperienced. The last thing either of them could afford was a war, but the two leaderships must have felt the pressure to demonstrate that they were in charge.

The British had left in a technical sense, but not quite in reality. Independent first Governor General was Lord

---

[15]'British Opposed Military Action in Kashmir: Advani', *Business Standard*, 7 November 2013, https://www.business-standard.com/article/news-ians/british-opposed-military-action-in-kashmir-advani-113110700938_1.html.

[16]'Nehru Was Reluctant to Send Troops to Kashmir: Advani', *Outlook*, 7 November 2013, https://www.outlookindia.com/newswire/story/nehru-was-reluctant-to-send-troops-to-kashmir-advani/816385.

Mountbatten and the commanders-in-chief of both armies were British nationals. The few remaining British officials must have had good channels of communication between themselves and certainly great averseness to a war as they were about to depart. Patel was a pragmatic leader who viewed the Hyderabad situation with great concern. As planning was his strength, Patel must have worked out alternatives and contingencies. By September 1948, Patel was impatient with the intransigence of the Nizam and started insisting that Operation Polo begin soon.

General Bucher was 53 years of age at the time of these events and probably looking forward to retiring from India and returning to his home country, which he did in early 1949. He had shown some signs of being an inflexible officer at the time of independence, when he passed an order that the public be kept away from flag hoisting. Nehru had to rescind that order and remind the general of the Indian government's supremacy.

General Bucher was at best hesitant, if not always opposed, to any army action in Hyderabad. For him, the disagreement was not a matter of ethics or principle; it was one of judgment on whether the nascent army could handle two difficult situations simultaneously. He probably had much to lose by supporting the police action, but little to lose by opposing it since his retirement was imminent.

When Patel took a firm line, General Bucher did not create any drama or resign, in fact, he ensured that the valid instructions (taken by the right people after listening to alternate views) be fully implemented. Though opposed to war, he was deeply conscious of the unreasonableness of the Nizam, as evidenced by his letter to his daughter six months before the police action. It could be said tha the real trouble in Hyderabad seemed to be that the Nizam had become bound hand and foot to the Ittehad.' Indian policy is one of reasonableness insofar as this is possible.'

Patel was very gracious towards General Bucher. After the successful Operation Polo, Patel wrote a letter of congratulation to him: 'I should like to send you and your officers and the men under their command my sincerest felicitations on the successful completion of the Hyderabad operations.'

∽

Analysis and Intuition

The absence of intuition—or its inadequate use—has the effect of constricting a manager. As a result, such managers are not able to work at their highest potential. A manager can develop to his full potential by learning to be intuitive, inclusive and humane—the kind of skills that are not taught. These skills are difficult to teach.

I have become sensitive to what cannot be taught, e.g., dealing with human nature, the complexities of employee behaviour within organizations, charting out an agenda for change. If a manager has failed to learn those lessons, it proves to be costly. Often, managers fail because they have not learnt such things. And these cannot be taught.

The reason why managers lean towards the analytical rather than the intuitive is because the analytical can be taught. Besides, patterns of career progression within companies also encourage this trend; people advance in their careers most often for being analytical, not for being intuitive. Analytical skills offer skill differentiation in the initial stages of one's career because these skills can be taught, they can be acquired by any willing student and what is available to any diligent learner soon ceases to be a sustainable differentiator.

It is not that analytics are unimportant or undesirable. They are essential. Top managers acknowledge that while taking decisions, they do place reliance on analysis and data, but ultimately, they are guided by their intuition. Experts and colleagues can analyse and comment. However, there is a limit as well as a limitation to analysis because of time, costs or techniques; that point is loosely referred to as the point of 'analysis paralysis'.

Managers know the limits of analysis, yet they transgress that limit and make mistakes. A common reason for managerial mistakes is that successful managers tend to repeat solutions that have previously worked for them or those that they think worked for other people. This is a valid approach when the problem and its solution are 'technical' in nature, for example, how to improve machine performance in a factory, or how to calculate the present value of a business with cash flow. In these 'technical' situations, both the problem and the solution are known.

Where 'human' factors are involved, neither the problem nor the solution is clearly known. The adoption of an earlier successful model may or may not work unless the context and circumstance of the two problem situations have been considered. Success in one human context does not necessarily transfer well onto another context.

Business history and entrepreneurship is full of stories about leaders who trusted their intuition.

The great Indian industrialist of the nineteenth century, Jamsetji Tata, had bought some marshy land near the Nagpur railway station in 1874 at a low price. He floated a firm called the Central India Spinning, Weaving and Manufacturing

Company. When asked to subscribe to its shares, a local Marwari banker refused to invest in support of a man who was wasting gold by sinking it into the ground. This person later admitted that Tata had put earth into the ground and pulled out gold.

In the 1950s, Ray Kroc decided to buy the McDonalds brand because his instinct kept urging him on. Against all odds, his company expanded to become an icon of fast food, not just in America, but all over the world.

In the late 1980s, ignoring all the market research evidence, Bob Lutz, then president of Chrysler, went ahead with the Dodge Viper car model. This was an outrageously powerful, eye-searing roadster launched at a time when Chrysler was down and out. Bob Lutz felt that the company had to take a lot of chances because it would go out of business if it did not. So he did a lot by intuition and cut out all the crap normally associated with a new product.

Knowledge, Intuition and Wisdom

Knowledge is what you know you know. Knowledge can be taught; you can acquire it from external sources.

Intuition is what you do not know you know. Intuition is what cannot be taught, you learn it on your own. At the core of intuition is a set of understandings that the owner just does not know about.

When knowledge is integrated with intuition, it becomes wisdom.

Both knowledge and intuition are valuable for leaders in their decision-making process. Is one more important than the other? Is one more desirable than the other? Not really, they are complementary in nature. Intuition plays a key role by filling in the blanks when there is not enough information.

The role and value of intuition increases as a person rises in the organization and finds that he has to solve more complex issues. In fact, such senior leaders are paid for their intuition: their knowledge is taken as a given.

Intuition does not always just 'happen'; it can be developed. The absence of intuition at crucial times is one of the reasons for the surprising failure of top leaders, who have established a reputation of success already. On the other hand, intuition must be learnt, and the way one uses it can be a huge differentiator. The absence of such intuitive qualities may explain the increasing management failures we see around us. However, there is a problem that managers face. It is not easy to teach intuition. It is not clear what exactly intuition is.

Intuition will be a key differentiator for excellence in the future, equal to or more than in the past. There are six simple messages:

- ◆ Intuition does exist and it is very important for the manager, especially at the more senior levels of leadership
- ◆ Analysis and intuition are not substitutes, they are complementary
- ◆ A manager can develop intuition through viewing issues holistically, with the 'surrounds' of the issues, and not in isolation. He should observe and learn from the peripherals of his vision, hearing, experiences and relationships
- ◆ The manager's intuition is enhanced through varied experiences and relationships, contemplation and reflection

♦ A manager can develop his intuition by exploring and sensing beyond what is visible and audible

♦ The leader needs to think about issues at the 'edges of the spectrum of the obvious'.

∞

The Hamlet Truth

In William Shakespeare's, *Hamlet*, Hamlet said to Horatio, 'There is a divinity that shapes our ends, rough hew them how you will.'[17] He was acknowledging that there were many things out of his control, and that in the end, it is God that will determine our destinies. The context was that the conflict in Hamlet's mind was causing him to lose sleep. You have surely had the experience of not being in control of events. Some people call the phenomenon God, while some others call it luck.

The reader may consider the inclusion of luck in this book to be unusual. The fact is that we believe in it in one sense and dismiss it in another sense. Accepting the existence of luck is perceived as a sign of weakness in our turbulent times. Luck can also become a crutch for non-performance. Therefore, organizations discourage any talk of luck. When positive things happen in an organization, leaders are quick to point out that it is the fruit of consciously adopted strategies and great foresight. When things go awry, the same leaders will readily cite external factors.

---

[17]William Shakespeare, *Hamlet*, Act V, Scene 2.

Author and academic, John Kay, criticizes the view that success in a business must be derived from a single, shaping vision or a mission statement that is relentlessly executed. It is wrong to imagine design when there was only adaptation and improvisation. It is wrong to attribute every success to some deliberate plan.

The same holds true for an individual's life. We are too easily misled by biographies of great people who, after the fact, claim to have meticulously planned their ascent. The origins of success are much too subtle and complex. Life does not follow a course and we change in many ways as we grow.

Adolf Hitler and Winston Churchill

On 22 August 1931, John Scott-Ellis, a young Englishman, was taking his new Fiat around Munich for a spin. As he drove up Ludwigstraße, he took a right turn into Brienner Straße, but a pedestrian crossed the road. He was knocked down. Scott-Ellis was reassured that he had not injured the pedestrian as the man picked himself up and walked away.

Three years later, Scott-Ellis, now 21 years of age, sat at the box office at Residentz Theatre. In the adjacent box sat the same man he had knocked down. The man recalled the incident but was 'quite charming for those few moments.' Later, Scott-Ellis realized that he had knocked down Adolf Hitler.

On 13 December 1931, an English politician was knocked down in New York's Fifth Avenue. The car was driving at 35 mph, a speed that could have killed him. The veteran MP was 57 years of age and was dragged several yards before being flung to one side. Churchill was rushed to Lenox Hill Hospital and he survived.

It is, of course, true that it is not a good way to lead your life by constantly relying on good luck coming your way or bad luck not crossing your path. Deep and disabling faith in luck can be hugely debilitating. Yet the complete denial of luck too is worth a reconsideration.

When you have prepared for an event, and the event goes your way, you can justifiably feel that you have earned that luck. For instance, you want that promotion to vice president; you slog hard and consistently deliver results as a general manager; you learn what there is to learn about the higher-level vice president's job. In other words, you develop yourself to a high state of preparedness. The current vice president retires, and you get the job. You have deserved the promotion, it is an earned luck, Quad Erat Demostrata (QED).

A slightly different case. You have done all that is stated above. But so has a colleague. It is clear to everyone that the promoted person will be one of you both. Some think you, and others think the other person. It is a close call. Three months before the current vice president retires, the other person dies in a car accident. You don't revel in his misfortune, but you become the beneficiary of unearned luck by becoming the single candidate for the bigger job. Unearned luck QED.

In my experience, luck matters, and admitting that it matters, matters even more—call it unearned luck if you will. It is true that you can miss reaping the benefits of unearned luck, but the fact remains that there is something called unearned luck.

I interviewed former Tata Sons director, Jamshed Jiji Irani, for one of my books. One of the subjects we both explored was Jamshed's idea of and acceptance of luck.

'Luck does not exist,' he said emphatically. 'You spin a coin for the cricket toss, then it is luck. But when you have prepared for an opportunity and your preparedness meets that opportunity, you grab it. Others may think it was luck, but I say, you prepared for it.'

As Jamshed talked about his early life and career, it became evident that there were coincidences that could be considered good luck or, at the very least, unearned luck. There were three unforeseen and unplanned interventions from a man whom he hardly knew at that point of time—J.R.D. Tata.

Jamshed recollected his student days in Nagpur in the 1950s. His father had worked in Tata Empress Mills and so did his future father-in-law. On his own merit, Jamshed won a Tata scholarship to study geology and metallurgy in England. His family could not have afforded to send him with their own finances. In one sense, winning that scholarship marked the beginning of his personal association with the house of Tata.

He reminisced, 'There was a formidable lady who used to select the Tata scholars, grill them and make sure that they stayed in contact. She would put up notes to J.R.D. Tata. As I was finishing my studies in England, it seems that J.R.D. had remarked that if ever this person wants to come back to India, ask him to first knock on the doors of Tata Iron and Steel Company (TISCO). That lady sent me the comment, stating that I should feel very proud that J.R.D. had said what he had said...as he rarely did so.' A bit of unearned luck or a coincidence, I wondered.

Jamshed did want to return to India and he did knock on the doors of TISCO. He was interviewed by J.R.D. Tata and Sumant Moolgaokar, initially in Mumbai. Later the director-in-charge, Nanavati, travelled to Sheffield and interviewed the young Jamshed in his office in England. An offer was made and Jamshed joined Jamshedpur in 1968 in the research department. As a safety net, he retained a lien on his job at British Steel for one year. He wanted to test how his professional life would shape up in TISCO.

The early period in Jamshedpur was not particularly enjoyable for Jamshed. He just did not enjoy the research job within his department. After several months of trying to find enjoyment in his job, he wrote to the company about his intention to return to his job in England. The bosses accepted his letter and Jamshed was all set to return.

And then another coincidence (or unearned luck?) happened.

J.R.D. was on an unplanned visit to Jamshedpur. He saw Jamshed along with a larger group of TISCO officers and enquired how 'the young man' was getting along. Jamshed was forthright in informing J.R.D. that he was not enjoying the job and that he had decided to return to England. All that J.R.D. said was, 'Oh,' and walked away. On the day after J.R.D. left Jamshedpur, three directors—Russi Mody, Nanavati and R.S. Pandey—summoned Jamshed to enquire why he was not enjoying his job. Upon listening to his reasons, they offered him an alternate role within the manufacturing department in the steel plant. This development must be attributed to J.R.D's intervention (unearned luck?). Jamshed felt he had met his challenge and started to enjoy his new role enormously, so much so that he started visualizing his long-term career ambition to reach the highest levels in TISCO.

Several years later, Jamshed was approached—without his seeking the opportunity—to join Steel Authority of India Limited (SAIL) as the chairman. In those days, joining the public sector was considered a nationalistic thing to do. Jamshed mentioned the SAIL offer to Russi Mody, who promptly reported the matter to J.R.D. J.R.D's response was something like, 'If Jamshed is even considering going to SAIL, then he must have his head examined because obviously he does not know the difference between Tata and SAIL!' Jamshed had anyway decided to stay at TISCO, but he counted this third intervention by J.R.D. as a fortuitous coincidence (or unearned luck).

I asked Jamshed about a more recent coincidence or unearned luck. Through whatever process of turmoil there was at the time, he was appointed as the CEO of TISCO in 1991. His appointment coincided with the country's national economic crisis. Liberalization and delicensing began with a bang under Prime Minister Narasimha Rao and Finance Minister Manmohan Singh. This unforeseen development gave Jamshed an unparalleled opportunity to reconstruct, renovate, modernize and downsize TISCO—all of which were badly needed moves. Had this development not occurred, Jamshed would have been yet another CEO of TISCO, who managed the government interface and steel price controls. Instead he could aspire to become—and he succeeded—the architect of setting TISCO on an entirely new and dynamic trajectory. Coincidence (or unearned luck?). 'Well, for sure, the liberalization was not influenced by me,' said Jamshed Irani wistfully.

When I was posted to Jeddah towards the end of 1990 as chairman, Unilever Arabia, war clouds were gathering over Saddam Hussein's belligerence with Kuwait. Many thought I was unlucky to be posted at such a time in what might become a war-ravaged geography. Indeed, on the morning of 12 January 1991, when I reported in London for my formal induction, the US Congress passed a joint resolution authorizing the use of military force to drive Iraq out of Kuwait. Operation Desert Storm had begun. Unilever director Chris Jemmett, my boss, welcomed me on that cold, bleary January day of 1991 with the cheerful words, 'Welcome, the war has begun.'

As I settled down to the tasks of the newly appointed chairman, travelling between London and Jeddah, the events of the war moved decisively. By 27 February 1991, US Marines and Saudi Arabian troops entered Kuwait City and engaged in what came to be known as the Battle of Medina Ridge. Within a few days, Kuwait accepted the UN ceasefire resolution. The war was over.

There was massive government spending after the war throughout the Gulf Cooperation Council states. The economy became buoyant and greatly helped me establish Unilever's Arabian business on a sound footing. Of course, there was earned luck insofar as Unilever had been preparing to invest in the geography for many years. But there was unearned luck insofar as the economic boom lifted Unilever's efforts with the rising tide. And I happened to be the chairman, it was luck for me, and of course, all my colleagues.

∽

Acknowledgements

We began this book with the anecdote about how the spaceship Voyager-1 photographed the receding earth as it drew away from earth six billion miles away. Writing this book has resembled that journey. Had we both not enjoyed the richness of our respective work experiences and learnt so much, we would never have thought of writing this book. We enjoyed the opportunity to reflect on our experiences after so many years.

We thank our publishers, Rupa, for their great commitment to bringing this book out. Mr Kapish Mehra was very enthusiastic about the concept and helped to shape its contours. Yamini Chowdhury was a relentless ally, enthusiastically connecting and guiding. We are grateful to the cover designer, the editing team and other allies in a publishing venture like this.

It must have been annoying for our spouses to see us so engrossed in the writing and debating process for such long periods. Gopalakrishnan would like to thank Geeta, Srinivasan would like to thank Mridula. We think they were both models of patience, but who knows? Maybe they were thankful that we were quite so preoccupied!

We never thought that we would write this book together.

We just followed our passion to share lessons and experiences. During our lives, most of us acquire some financial wealth, which we are reluctant to part with. We also acquire considerably more experiential wealth, which we are happy to part with, if only there are takers. We all should die and can do so if our experiential assets have been shared widely.

We think we will leave a little bit of ourselves and our life lessons through this book.

We were hesitant, at first, because we thought that our experiences were commonplace. How could they be of interest to anybody? And even if they were, of what value would they be? Through serendipitous verbal duels, debate and differences, we started to shape the concept of this book. As co-authors, we must thank each other, even if it appears gratuitous and unnecessary.

R. Gopalakrishnan
R. Srinivasan

Index